Increasing the Teaching Role of Academic Libraries

Thomas G. Kirk, *Editor*

NEW DIRECTIONS FOR TEACHING AND LEARNING
KENNETH E. EBLE, *Editor-in-Chief*

Number 18, June 1984

Paperback sourcebooks in
The Jossey-Bass Higher Education Series

Jossey-Bass Inc., Publishers
San Francisco • Washington • London

Thomas G. Kirk (Ed.).
Increasing the Teaching Role of Academic Libraries.
New Directions for Teaching and Learning, no. 18.
San Francisco: Jossey-Bass, 1984.

New Directions for Teaching and Learning Series
Kenneth E. Eble, *Editor-in-Chief*

New Directions for Teaching and Learning is published quarterly
by Jossey-Bass Inc., Publishers. Subscriptions, single-issue
orders, change of address notices, undelivered copies, and other
correspondence should be sent to Subscriptions, Jossey-Bass Inc.,
Publishers, 433 California Street, San Francisco, California 94104.

Editorial correspondence should be sent to the Editor-in-Chief,
Kenneth E. Eble, Department of English, University of Utah,
Salt Lake City, Utah 84112.

Library of Congress Catalogue Card Number LC 83-82744

International Standard Serial Number ISSN 0271-0633

International Standard Book Number ISBN 87589-791-6

Cover art by Willi Baum

Manufactured in the United States of America

Ordering Information

The paperback sourcebooks listed below are published quarterly and can be ordered either by subscription or single-copy.

Subscriptions cost $35.00 per year for institutions, agencies, and libraries. Individuals can subscribe at the special rate of $25.00 per year *if payment is by personal check.* (Note that the full rate of $35.00 applies if payment is by institutional check, even if the subscription is designated for an individual.) Standing orders are accepted. Subscriptions normally begin with the first of the four sourcebooks in the current publication year of the series. When ordering, please indicate if you prefer your subscription to begin with the first issue of the *coming* year.

Single copies are available at $8.95 when payment accompanies order, and *all single-copy orders under $25.00 must include payment.* (California, New Jersey, New York, and Washington, D.C., residents please include appropriate sales tax.) For billed orders, cost per copy is $8.95 plus postage and handling. (Prices subject to change without notice.)

Bulk orders (ten or more copies) of any individual sourcebook are available at the following discounted prices: 10–49 copies, $8.05 each; 50–100 copies, $7.15 each; over 100 copies, *inquire.* Sales tax and postage and handling charges apply as for single copy orders.

To ensure correct and prompt delivery, all orders must give either the *name of an individual* or an *official purchase order number.* Please submit your order as follows:

Subscriptions: specify series and year subscription is to begin.
Single Copies: specify sourcebook code (such as, TL8) and first two words of title.

Mail orders for United States and Possessions, Latin America, Canada, Japan, Australia, and New Zealand to:
    Jossey-Bass Inc., Publishers
    433 California Street
    San Francisco, California 94104

Mail orders for all other parts of the world to:
    Jossey-Bass Limited
    28 Banner Street
    London EC1Y 8QE

New Directions for Teaching and Learning Series
Kenneth E. Eble, *Editor-in-Chief*

Contents

Editor's Notes

A quiet revolution has occurred in academic libraries. The professional focus of academic libraries has shifted from a passive and, at best, responsive role to an active involvement in the educational program of the institution. This change has occurred in response to a variety of forces at work in the educational program of the institution. These forces include:

1. The proliferating volume of information and the consequent inability of the individual to maintain knowledgeable control over any substantial portion of it,
2. The changed nature of educational programs that places greater emphasis on individualized work by students,
3. The changed nature of educational programs that places greater emphasis on preparing students for a life of continuing education,
4. The rapid change within disciplines that requires continual contact with the current literature of the field, and
5. The increasing use of automated systems that requires sophisticated skills to retrieve information effectively.

The quiet revolution that has occurred in academic libraries has resulted in the development of programs of bibliographic or library instruction. The term *library instruction* may invoke images of library tours and explanations of the card catalogue and *Reader's Guide*. However, in today's programs these are but a first step and only a small portion of the service an academic library can offer in a program of bibliographic or library instruction. The chapters in this volume reflect the tremendous diversity and scope of activities that fall under the purview of a bibliographic or library instruction program. All of these activities have as their goal "to help individuals develop the intellectual and manipulative skills needed for the retrieval, assimilation, and critical analysis of . . . information" (Association of College and Research Libraries, 1979, p. 5).

This volume is intended to provide a compact overview of the expanding area of library service. In Chapter One, the concept of library service is explained, and then the development of the concept is reviewed in Chapter Two. The conceptual and pedagogical issues with which librarians are struggling are treated in Chapters Three and Four. Two other chapters deal with particularly difficult issues: Chapter Five tells how to find library use assignments that can serve as alternatives to the term paper, and Chapter Six explores ways to gain faculty support. Chapter Seven provides a survey of the leading programs. The invisible college that is centered around the LOEX information exchange is explained in Chapter Eight. Readers are introduced to the extensive literature on the subject of bibliographic instruction in Chapter Nine. Finally, the question of why a bibliographic instruction program is necessary is addressed in the concluding chapter.

Thomas G. Kirk
Editor

Reference

Association of College and Research Libraries, Bibliographic Instruction Section. *Bibliographic Instruction Handbook*. Chicago: Association of College and Research Libraries, 1979.

Thomas G. Kirk has been college librarian at Berea College since 1980. Previously he served as science librarian at Earlham College from 1965 to 1980.

*Bibliographic instruction is a significant service offered
by the teaching library.*

Teaching, Research, and Service: The Academic Library's Role

Carla J. Stoffle
Alan E. Guskin
Joseph A. Boisse

Since the turn of the century, the library has been acknowledged in almost every college and university by faculty, students, and administrators as the "heart of the campus" (Rothstein, 1955). Yet on most campuses, the educational and community service potential of the library is largely unrealized. The library and its staff are devoted to collecting, organizing, and preserving materials. This is a passive role that causes the library to be viewed, somewhat appropriately, by campus administration as an underutilized, expensive storehouse. In this view, the library is considered a place where students socialize or study for class assignments but rarely do research, leisure reading, or non-course related learning. Regardless of the resources invested, the passive library rarely satisfies the faculty. Frequently, the faculty (and sometimes students and university administrators as well) consider academic librarians in these libraries as "keepers of the books" or, in the words of a Cambridge University faculty member, "warehouse managers" (Cubbin, 1980) rather than as partners who have considerable resources and expertise to contribute to the teaching, service, and research missions of the institution. Given the substantial investment that institutions make in libraries and the current demands and

T. G. Kirk (Ed.). *Increasing the Teaching Role of Academic Libraries.*
New Directions for Teaching and Learning, no. 18. San Francisco: Jossey-Bass, June 1984.

challenges faced by higher education, the unfulfilled potential of the academic library is unfortunate and unnecessary.

How academic libraries and librarians can help their institutions face the educational and service challenges of the 1980s is the focus of this chapter.

Major Issues in Higher Education

Much has been written about the fiscal crisis facing higher education. Almost every new issue of *The Chronicle of Higher Education* describes yet another institution that is suffering from budget cuts due to lowered state appropriations or decreased resources due to shortfalls in enrollment. In the last few years, it has become painfully clear that support for higher education has become a lower priority for the general public and that the value of a college education is being seriously questioned (Astin, 1981). Obviously, the state of the economy, the decline in enrollments projected as the result of fewer eighteen- to twenty-two-year-olds, and competition for public dollars by the military and by social programs has much to do with the amount of funding being made available for education. These are not, however, the only reasons that support has declined. The public has lost confidence in higher education institutions and their potential for serving society's needs. This loss of confidence, due partly to the disappointment and anger over student unrest of the 1960s and 1970s, is also a product of the poor performance and lack of achievement of colleges and universities in the public service arena and in maintaining the quality of undergraduate education over the last two decades.

In the 1960s, higher education was called upon to exercise its service mission, that is, to apply its special knowledge and expertise to the solution of the problems of the society at large (Corson, 1975). Many institutions responded and became involved. Vast sums of money were made available for the development of solutions to social problems such as unemployment, social welfare, urban housing, organized crime, race relations, water and air pollution, and education (Re, 1969). In the 1980s, there is little public faith that higher education can solve these problems; either higher education oversold its potential or the public expected more than was realistic. However, now the challenge for many institutions is to find ways to rebuild the public trust and to develop appropriate service programs for their communities. The alternative is for higher education to learn to exist on much less funding and for society to be limited in the resources available for dealing with its problems.

A second major challenge for higher education is to provide open access yet maintain academic standards. Open admissions and increased access to higher education are laudable social goals. But for institutions to provide open access and a quality education without becoming a revolving door will require university resources, creative programming, and the commitment of the entire institution. This will be a difficult, long-term task, especially in light of predictions that the skills of most high school graduates in the United States will not reach minimal college entrance standards until well into the 1990s (Roueche, 1981).

A related challenge facing many colleges and universities is the increasing diversity of the student population. Adult and part-time students are projected to become the majority groups on many four-year campuses. These students will be on campus less but will demand more of the university in terms of the type and quality of education and educational services they require. Because of their commitments to home, work, and community activities, these students will have limited time for their education. They will, therefore, need more flexible course scheduling than their younger, full-time counterparts as well as more challenging assignments and better and more integrated services.

To meet the challenges of the 1980s — restoration of public trust, maintenance of access and high standards, and adaptation to an increasingly diverse student body — colleges and universities and their constituent units will need leadership with vision, creativity, flexibility, tenacity, and commitment. This leadership will be required from individuals or groups that have academic or educational credibility and a broad concept of the role of higher education.

The Teaching Library

As the symbolic heart of the campus and the academic unit which interacts with the entire campus community, academic libraries have the potential for exercising considerable influence and leadership in the institution's adjustment to and meeting of current challenges. However, to do this academic libraries must direct their goals and activities away from that of merely collecting, organizing, and preserving materials. Libraries must adopt a broader conceptualization of the role of the academic library. One appropriate role model is that of the teaching library. A teaching library is a library that is more than a support unit for academic programs and research. It is a library that is actively and directly involved in advancing all aspects of the mission of instructions of higher education: teaching, research, and community service (Guskin and others, 1979). Generally a teaching library is characterized by commitment to:

1. Instructing students, faculty, and staff in the effective identification and use of information resources,

2. Developing a climate which encourages life-long learning and develops an awareness of the need for continuing education beyond the classroom among the members of both the on- and off-campus communities,

3. Maintaining a library collection that supports and stimulates inquiry into areas outside the curriculum as well as supporting teaching and research,

4. Sharing resources in a way that provides easy access to materials not available in the library,

5. Making the library a cultural center for the campus and community,
6. Providing access to and encouraging the apppropriate use of its resources by residents in the surrounding communities, and
7. Conducting research that will help improve library services and its bibliographic system.

While not all teaching libraries have all these commitments, the missions of those libraries that have accepted the teaching library concept reflect many of these goals.

The core component of the teaching library is a comprehensive bibliographic instruction program. The purpose of a bibliographic instruction program is to teach students, and sometimes faculty, how to effectively find, evaluate, and use information (Tuckett and Stoffle, 1983; Kirkendall and Stoffle, 1982). The instructional methods used vary but may take the form of more lectures to classes with library-related assignments; separate courses, both credit and noncredit; and workshops. The materials for such programs include, among others: simple bibliographies, self-paced manuals (patterned after the lab manuals used in the sciences), computer assisted instruction software, video tapes, and slide tapes (Stoffle and Bonn, 1973).

A comprehensive program of bibliographic instruction has three components: (1) a general orientation to available facilities and resources, (2) the teaching of basic research skills and strategies, and (3) the teaching of the organization of the literature in various disciplines as well as the basic reference tools in each discipline. In addition, the program should be characterized by: (1) a written profile identifying the audiences requiring instruction and their needs, (2) a written statement of instructional goals and objectives, and (3) a plan for evaluating the instructional program (American Library Association, 1977).

The development of a successful bibliographic instruction program requires that teaching faculty and professional librarians engage in frequent contact and view each other as partners in the educational enterprise. It requires collaboration about course content, requirements and assignments; frequent discussion of materials available or needed in the library; and joint review of what students need to be taught about using the library to successfully complete course assignments.

While a comprehensive bibliographic instruction program is essential in a teaching library, it is not the sole component. A variety of other activities, many of which are not new to academic libraries, will be found in a teaching library. However, in a teaching library, these activities have been developed on the basis of the library's overall goals and commitments and are grounded in the library's commitment to advance the teaching, research, and community service missions of the parent institution.

Services that may result from those commitments to enriching the climate of learning on campus, generating greater use of library resources, and contributing to the general education of both the on- and off-campus communities might include:

1. Campus displays of library materials on topics of current interest nationally, locally, or to the campus,
2. Displays and book exhibits from outside sources that represent a variety of perspectives and that stimulate students to investigate new areas of thought,
3. Regular showings of educational or cultural films and videotapes during lunch hours or at other times and when students are likely to be out of classes,
4. Special areas for recreational reading, with availability of popular fiction and nonfiction book collections and display of both traditional and avant garde artwork,
5. Sponsorship of lectures, poetry readings, and so on either in the library or at other locations on campus, and
6. Bulletin boards displaying notices of cultural activities on and off campus, book reviews, film reviews, and so on.

From its commitment to providing access to and encouraging the use of its collections by community residents, the library staff may: (1) develop book lists or bibliographies describing the resources of the library in areas of interest to community agencies or special interest groups, (2) establish special circulation privileges for community agencies, schools, and businesses, (3) issue library cards to community residents to allow them the same circulation and use privileges as students, (4) make available access to on-line computerized data base searches, (5) provide on-site and telephone reference and information services, and (6) prepare public programs designed to stimulate the use of humanities or special collections (Josey, 1975, 1976, 1977, 1979, 1980; Virgo, 1981).

A logical extension of the commitments of the teaching library is that the library provide library instruction to the community at large. Academic librarians may become involved in precollegiate programs designed to improve high school student skills and to stimulate these students to prepare for college. In addition, librarians may provide instructional sessions or in-service workshops on locating and using the specialized materials available in academic libraries for such local groups as government employees, area business people, professionals in local social service agencies, teachers, and members of community organizations (such as historical societies).

Other community-related activities of the teaching library may include programs coordinated with other area libraries or agencies. Such programs may include traditional resource sharing activities or may involve the cosponsoring of film programs and lectures, the preparation and sharing of displays, the publication of specialized magazines, and the development of unique information files with reference to community resources, both material and human (Galloway and Horn, 1975; Josey, 1978).

Because of its commitments, the staff of the teaching library is genuinely concerned with collection development. This concern begins with the need to provide materials that support the curriculum and faculty research. It extends to the library's special function within the institution: to provide general reading materials, materials presenting alternative views on topics of social concern (Galloway and Horn, 1975), and materials which stimulate inquiry into areas outside the coverage of the curriculum (American Library Association, 1975, 1982; Farber, 1981). This function of the teaching library makes an important contribution to the fulfillment of the responsibility that all libraries have to foster and encourage reading and to help prepare an informed citizenry.

To fulfill the library's collection commitments requires that librarians develop a carefully constructed collection policy. In addition, they must work with faculty in selection to ensure that those materials that are likely to be used are purchased. Finally, it is important that librarians and faculty work with university administrators to ensure their awareness of the importance of the library collection to the teaching and learning process as well as faculty research.

Because individual academic libraries are unlikely to be able to purchase all the materials that would be useful, the teaching library is especially committed to the establishment of fast, efficient, and effective resource sharing mechanisms. The librarians in these institutions devote substantial resources in support of local, state, and national resource sharing systems and provide extensive collections of reference materials including on-line computerized data bases to help the user identify the resources available regardless of their location. In addition, interlibrary loan and computerized searching are made available free to institutional members and at minimal cost to community residents so that access to information and quality research work are not based solely on an ability to pay.

As the result of all of the aforementioned commitments, the professional staff of the teaching library is engaged in research that will lead to the improvement of library services and the increased ability of libraries to make materials accessible. This research may take many forms: citation analyses of published literature used by faculty members, studies of how and why students do or do not use the academic library, analyses of architectural impacts on library use, evaluations of the effectiveness of the various methods of instruction for teaching students how to use the library, preparation and publication of scholarly bibliographies, and studies of the impact of the new technology on library services and users.

Creating a Teaching Library: The Process

Creating a teaching library is not a simple task. It takes careful planning, flexibility, commitment, and skill on the part of the library staff. A teaching library requires a staff that (1) understands and accepts the commitments of the teaching library, (2) thinks in terms of jobs that need to be done rather than merely time commitments, (3) is active in continuing education and professional association activities, (4) views teaching as important, (5) is oriented to people, and (6) is committed to engaging in research—library as well as faculty research.

The role of the director in implementing a teaching library is especially critical. A director is needed who will: (1) foster an environment that encourages staff risk taking and creativity; (2) hire, train, and reward staff members who are able to accept the challenge of creating a teaching library; (3) be a successful advocate with faculty and senior administrators for support and resources; and (4) redirect, if necessary, current library resources to support teaching library programs.

The development of a successful teaching library also depends on the faculty and administration. Faculty members who care about teaching, are rewarded for good teaching and public service, and are flexible enough to accept the library and librarians in new roles are key components. Also needed are support and encouragement from senior level administrators. This support must include: (1) providing necessary fiscal resources, (2) approving the new goals and priorities of the library, (3) providing a climate that encourages risk taking on the part of faculty and staff, and (4) providing moral support for the library's activities by highlighting them on campus and in surrounding communities.

The actual process of creating a teaching library should begin with an analysis by the library staff of the internal and external environmental factors directly affecting the campus. The analysis should involve the examination of institutional goals and objectives, priorities, curriculum, long-range plans, and any other factors that are likely to substantially affect the future of the institution. Following the environmental analysis, the populations who will be served and their educational and informational needs should be identified. These populations may include undergraduates, graduate students, faculty, area high school students, teachers, businessmen, city officials, and so forth. Who the library ultimately serves is a function of the institution's commitments and the commitments and creativity of the library staff.

When assessing the populations and their needs, the library staff should also analyze the library resources that can be utilized in teaching library programs. Most critical is the assessment of the available human resources: the commitment and ability of the library director to implement the teaching library in terms of technical expertise, internal leadership skills, and influence on senior administrators; and the skill of the present library staff to implement the array of programs that make up a teaching library while not losing sight of the need to collect, organize, preserve, and make available library materials. This last consideration is extremely important because students, faculty, university administrators, and community residents will reject the teaching library programs if books do not get reshelved quickly and correctly, if materials are not ordered in a timely fashion, if the library does not have sufficient materials to meet core campus needs, if staff are not available to answer reference questions, if interlibrary loans take unreasonable lengths of time, or if new materials are not processed and made available within a reasonable time period.

Besides the ability and availability of staff, the library resource assessment should include consideration of the finances available to the library. Additionally, the potential for the reallocation of library funds to new programs must be examined with the fiscal resources within the university. Also, the needs of the collection must be analyzed and the capability of fulfilling them must be realistically assessed. Finally, the availability of equipment for present and future needs and the potential for support from consortial relationships with other libraries and community agencies must be explored.

Once the assessment of the environment, the populations to be served, and the available resources has been completed, goals and objectives for the teaching library must be established. The importance of clearly defined goals and objectives cannot be emphasized too strongly. In the process of developing goals and objectives, library staff will gain a clearer understanding of their own self-interests, the university's interests, their conceptions of a library generally and of a teaching library specifically, as well as what can and should be accomplished. A critical element in the development of goals and objectives is the process itself. Faculty, staff, students, and appropriate community members should be involved in the discussions. Through participation, these individuals and groups will not only contribute constructive insights but will also become committed to the outcome. Obviously, the development of a commitment will depend on the sincerity with which the consultation takes place; if the process is open and has the potential to produce changes, involvement in the development of goals and objectives will likely lead participants to understand the teaching library and to support its implementation. This type of consultation is especially important in periods of fiscal constraint since the development of some of the programs in the teaching library may displace other more established library activities.

Once goals and objectives are established, programs and activities must be carefully designed to implement them. This program development step must take place within the context of the resource analyses and needs assessments steps previously completed. Program design is primarily the responsibility of library staff but must be carried out with the collaboration of faculty and administrators. Because each university has a unique configuration of internal and external resources and needs, the nature and type of programs that emerge will be distinctive.

Developing an evaluation component should follow the decision about which programs and activities to implement. The purpose of evaluation is to provide the library with a method for improving its programs, redirecting them when necessary, changing them when appropriate, and discontinuing them when they have served their purpose.

Creating the Teaching Library: The Problems

Some problems that can arise when redirecting the library from a passive to an active role have been touched on in the preceding discussion. There are, in addition, several other major problems. The first of these concerns the education of academic librarians. Most academic librarians have not received the professional preparation necessary to successfully operate in a teaching library environment. Much of library education for academic librarians is focused on the memorization of the titles, organization, and contents of hundreds of reference books, on learning how to catalogue books, on developing administrative skills, and on coping with the automation of libraries. Little or no attention is given to the possible roles of higher education, the organization and governance of colleges and universities, and the role of the academic library in the university (Josey and Blake, 1970). In addition, academic librarians are not generally taught about assessing the needs of the institution or clientele, goal setting, or introducing innovations in educational institutions. Finally, the majority of academic librarians are not trained to teach or do research or to even understand that teaching and research are basic functions of the library (Galloway, 1976).

Another major problem inherent in implementing a teaching library is that faculty do not accept librarians as colleagues; consequently, librarians have a minor role in governance (Marchant, 1969). Most librarians do not have faculty rank since the library degree is an M.A. or M.S., although some librarians do have additional master's degrees or Ph.D.s. Even on those campuses where librarians have faculty rank and status, they rarely are treated as colleagues and have little or no impact on the running of the institution, especially in the curriculum area. This may be because many faculty members have never experienced, even as students, the benefits of working with librarians in a teaching library context (Farber, 1974). The potential intrusion of another academic professional into the classroom can be threatening as well (Farber, 1978). Whatever the reason for faculty's reluctance to accept librarians as equals, it is clear that this alone can prevent the successful implementation of a teaching library. In institutions where faculty and librarian relations are already strained, the first priority of librarians must be to build bridges to increase the understanding of the faculty.

Benefits of a Teaching Library

Although there are major problems and hurdles to be overcome in developing the totality of the teaching library, there are myriad potential benefits. Students benefit from increased skills that lead to greater confidence, improved performance on assignments requiring library research, and enhanced learning from curricular activities. In addition, students with information gathering skills are equipped to be life-long learners and are able to explore personal, intellectual, and recreational interests outside the classroom. Finally, because of the teaching library's wide ranging programs and activities that are designed to stimulate student learning on topics not covered by the curriculum, students receive a broader education than they might otherwise.

Faculty benefit from the programs of the teaching library in multiple ways. The close collaboration between faculty and librarians required to successfully implement the concept of the teaching library leads to greater library awareness of and support for faculty research and teaching. In addition, faculty members find that curriculum and course development are facilitated by working with librarians who know the collection, who are skilled educators, and who are prepared to assist in the development and implementation of research assignments. The involvement of librarians in the teaching and learning process also provides the faculty with feedback on student performance and problems as the students are engaged in their assignments. This feedback enables faculty to maximize learning opportunities by making adjustments during the learning process. Another benefit of the instructional activities of the library, as observed by one faculty member (Canary, 1978) in an institution that has implemented the teaching library concept, is that:

> Advanced instruction... can bring alternative [instructional] models into the classrooms of faculty in a variety of disciplines. Because it is almost inevitably a collaborative enterprise, it can involve faculty members in new modes [of instruction]; it thus offers some of the advantages of team teaching at much less expense... It should be noted that library instruction... is an area particularly open to alternative [instruction methods].... Library instruction can serve as a "carrier" for mediated instruction, computer assisted instruction, unit mastery systems, and other instructional forms....When you have a full discipline working together with a librarian, people can be acquiring new teaching ideas and techniques without even knowing they are improving their teaching [pp. 40–41].

The teaching library also enriches the lives of community residents who have access to its resources and services. Individually, residents are able to utilize the vast resources of an academic library for personal or professional development. Access to such resources increases the potential for improved services and performance in both the private and public sector. In addition, the community gains when high schools and colleges work together to provide educational opportunities designed to improve the skills of secondary school students. Finally, the cooperation between all types of libraries and public agencies and the academic library provides a stimulating cultural and intellectual environment in the community and maximizes the potential return on public dollars expended.

Colleges and universities have much to gain from the programs and services of a teaching library. The active involvement of the library in the academic programs of the institution leads to increased student skills and improved faculty productivity. These, in turn, lead to the enahancement of the quality of the educational programs of the institutions. In addition, the programs of the teaching library help the institution in its efforts to retain as well as recruit high quality faculty and students. The community activities of the library result in improved relations with the community and increased public confidence in the academic standards and quality of the institution. In institutions where librarians have implemented their responsibilities, a configuration of programs and activities known as the teaching library emerges and the library and the librarians become a powerful campus force helping the institution adapt to the changing demands of society.

References

American Library Association, Association of College and Research Libraries, Bibliographic Instruction Task Force. "Guidelines for Bibliographic Instruction in Academic Libraries." *College and Research Libraries News,* 1977, *38,* 92.

Astin, A. W. "The Dangerous Myth of Overeducation." *Chronicle of Higher Education,* 1981, *23,* 56.

Canary, R. "Library Instruction as a Model for Educational Innovation." Paper presented at the Leadership Conference on Bibliographic Instruction, University of Wisconsin at Parkside, June 22–24, 1978.

Corson, J. J. *The Governance of Colleges and Universities.* New York: McGraw-Hill, 1975.

Cubbin, G. "Fresh Priorities in Library User Education." In P. Fox (Ed.), *Library User Education: Are New Approaches Needed?* Proceedings of a conference at Trinity College, Cambridge, 1979. The British Library Research and Development Reports, Report No. 5503. London: British Library Research and Development Department, 1980.

Farber, E. I. "College Librarians and the University-Library Syndrome." In E. I. Farber and R. Walling (Eds.), *The Academic Librarian: Essays in Honor of Guy R. Lyle.* Metuchen, N.J.: Scarecrow Press, 1974.

Farber, E. I. "Librarian-Faculty Communication Techniques." In C. Oberman-Soroka (Ed.), *On Approaches to Bibliographic Instruction: Proceedings of Southeastern Conference.* Charleston, S.C.: College of Charleston, 1978.

Farber, E. I. "Collection Development from a College Perspective: A Comment." In W. Miller and D. S. Rockwood (Eds.), *College Librarianship.* Metuchen, N.J.: Scarecrow Press, 1981.

Galloway, R. D., and Horn, Z. "Alternative Ways to Meet User Needs." In E. J. Josey (Ed.), *New Dimensions for Academic Library Science.* Metuchen, N. J.: Scarecrow Press, 1975.

Galloway, S. "Nobody Is Teaching the Teachers." *Booklegger,* 1976, *3,* 29–31.

Guskin, A. E., Stoffle, C. J., and Boisse, J. A. "The Academic Library as a Teaching Library: A Role for the 1980s." *Library Trends,* 1979, *28,* 281–296.

Josey, E. J. "Social Responsibilities." In *ALA Yearbook.* Chicago: American Library Association, 1975, 1976, 1977, 1978, 1979, 1980.

Josey, E. J., and Blake, F. M. "Educating the Academic Librarian." *Library Journal,* 1970, *95,* 125–130.

Kirkendall, C. A., and Stoffle, C. J. "Instruction." In G. Schlacter (Ed.), *The Service Imperative.* Littleton, Colo.: Libraries Unlimited, 1982.

14

Marchant, M. P. "Faculty-Librarian Conflict." *Library Journal,* 1969, *94,* 2886–2889.

Re, E. D. "Education in the Nation's Service." In C. G. Dobbins and C. B. T. Lee (Eds.), *Whose Goals for American Higher Education?* Washington, D.C.: American Council on Education, 1969.

Rothstein, S. *The Development of Reference Services.* ACRL Monographs, No. 14. Chicago: Association of College and Research Libraries, 1955.

Roueche, J. E. "Holistic Literacy in College Teaching." Keynote Speech, Third Basic Skills Conference, University of Wisconsin at Parkside, Kenosha, Wisconsin, October, 1981.

Stoffle, C. J., and Bonn, G. "An Inventory of Library Orientation and Instruction Methods, *RQ,* 1973, *13,* 129–133.

Tuckett, H., and Stoffle, C. J. "Library Instruction: Toward User Self-Reliance." *Catholic Library World,* 1983, *54* (9), forthcoming.

Virgo, J. "Humanities Proposals for Academic Libraries." Program Proposal to NEH Public Programs Division, Association of College and Research Libraries, 1981.

Carla J. Stoffle has been assistant chancellor for Educational Services at the University of Wisconsin, Parkside, since 1979. Currently she is a doctoral candidate at the University of Wisconsin, Madison. Before entering university administration she held a variety of library positions at the University of Kentucky, Eastern Kentucky University, and University of Wisconsin, Parkside.

Alan E. Guskin is chancellor at University of Wisconsin, Parkside.

Joseph A. Boisse is director of libraries at Temple University.

Notions of what it means to be liberally educated, suggested by Ralph Waldo Emerson and amplified by academic librarians in the latter part of the nineteenth century, continue to stimulate the development of concepts of bibliographic instruction.

Emerson's Library Legacy: Concepts of Bibliographic Instruction

John Mark Tucker

To understand concepts of bibliographic instruction as they developed historically, one must consider nineteenth-century philosopher Ralph Waldo Emerson's observations about higher education. Emerson criticized colleges for providing libraries while furnishing no "professor of books," and he added that "no chair is so much wanted" (Emerson, 1858, p. 344). Although representing a quantum leap in the emergence of ideas about bibliographic instruction, the phrase, "professor of books," remains elusive, and it symbolizes the central problem generally recognized by librarians who teach students how to use libraries: that bibliographic instruction has always suffered from an inadequately formed theoretical or conceptual framework. The professor of books concept is one idea in the history of ideas on the topic. The present chapter, while treating the growth of the concepts of bibliographic instruction, is primarily a history of the ideas, notions, terms, and phrases about it.

The Professor of Books Concept

McMullen (1955) traces the idea of the professor of books to Emerson's lectures in the 1840s, some thirty years before American universities began

T. G. Kirk (Ed.). *Increasing the Teaching Role of Academic Libraries.*
New Directions for Teaching and Learning, no. 18. San Francisco: Jossey-Bass, June 1984.

emerging as research institutions. In the latter part of the nineteenth century, a number of academic librarians were inspired by Emerson's notion, and they tried to amplify it with their own ideas, drawn chiefly from the liberal arts tradition (Perkins, 1876; Bisbee, 1897). They believed that college students should acquire the intelligent use of books as an essential attribute of any well-educated person. Addressing themselves specifically to the undergraduate curriculum, Raymond C. Davis (1886) and Charles B. Shaw (1928) argued that students should be taught bibliography just as they are taught literature, art, or philosophy. Azariah Smith Root planned his courses for the "immediate benefit to the student in his future college work" (Oberlin College, 1903, p. 91).

As graduates of small liberal arts colleges, these professors and librarians were imbued with a commitment to the importance of being liberally educated, and they saw the professor of books as the one rightly chosen to help maintain this tradition. A consistent theme throughout the development of the idea of bibliographic instruction is that it is essential to the well-rounded college graduate. The liberal arts imperative of bibliographic instruction has currently found support among many others (Shores, 1964; Knapp, 1966; Broadus, 1967; and Tucker, 1981); in the mid-twentieth century, it was still occasionally embodied in the terms, "professor of books" or "professor of bibliography," which have served as official titles in a few libraries (McMullen, 1955, p. 161).

Bibligraphic instruction is permeated by another Emersonian principle of liberal education, that of great respect for human intellect, creativity, and curiosity. This principle places highest priority on the student's individuality and independence of thought (Maddock, 1957; Wayman, 1936). A number of librarians manifested this ideal by urging that students should be taught in a way that would enable them to read and study productively after their formal education had ended. Their skills would be due to their college-acquired facility to handle library resources with ease (Little, 1893; Poole, 1893). Poole (1893) also underscored the importance of independence in research. Students, he noted, should be able to teach themselves, to define their own interests, to pursue those interests with clarity of thought, and to exercise critical judgment independent of their former instructors. Books themselves were the best teachers. Though no longer formally affiliated with a college or university, properly educated graduates needed only to be near a good library in order to use books independently throughout their lives.

Bibliographic Instruction in the Context of Higher Education

Theories of teaching library use have usually depended on the overall educational purposes served by colleges and universities. Accordingly, bibliographic instruction followed the major movements characteristic of higher education in the latter nineteenth century. These movements, which significantly shaped present-day academe, may be summarized as the pedagogical ideals of liberal culture, research, and utility (Veysey, 1965).

The concepts of research and utility took root in the United States in the 1870s. However, liberal culture, also known as general culture or liberal education (Veysey, 1965) is centuries old, having philosophical precedents in ancient Greece. The basic notions of liberal culture are that education frees human intellect, brings to the fore innate human potential, and requires that the person function as an informed citizen with responsibilities to the body politic (Brubcher, 1977). Thus, according to the concepts of liberal culture, persons should not only be educated to possess knowledge and to accomplish tasks, but also to realize their human potential. These sentiments continue to influence undergraduate education and the meaning of a liberal education.

In the centuries since the emergence of Greek culture, liberal education has had broader and more varied manifestation, notably in the medieval university with its emphasis on the *trivium* and *quadrivium* and in universities of the nineteenth century whose purposes have been defined by philosopher John Henry Newman.

Newman (1959 [1853]) related his definition of liberal education to his definition of knowledge, which he saw as "taking a view of things" (p. 138). Knowledge was much more than merely information, and obtaining knowledge involved more than merely the process of acquisition. Knowledge was seen as inherently intellectual; to obtain it involved reasoning about and understanding what was perceived through the senses. Knowledge should be considered irrespective of its results, so that it could be viewed as an end in itself. Its value lay in its nature as a scientific or philosophical process.

A further aspect of knowledge was the notion of enlargement (Newman, 1959 [1853]). Just as knowledge was seen as taking a view of things, so learning or enlargement of the intellect involved comparing points-of-view. No enlargement would occur without a comparison of ideas. Thus, the mere acquisition of facts could not constitute a liberal education. The enlargement aspect of liberal learning was viewed as a process of taking in, considering, processing, systematizing, and comparing facts and ideas. This aspect was considered essential to a liberal education. Into this tradition of liberal learning, librarians introduced Emersonian ideas, and it was this tradition that they sought to improve and enhance through bibliographic instruction.

Academic librarians of the latter part of the nineteenth century developed a concept of the library and their role as librarians that was inherently pedagogical. For the most part, they were untrained in library science. (Professional library education did not begin in the United States until 1887, and most library schools did not affiliate with universities until the 1920s. Thus, it was well into the twentieth century before library schools produced graduates who had both been introduced to a body of theoretical knowledge about librarianship and who undertook their studies in an environment of academic scholarship.) Rather, these librarians were professors who had obtained library posts for various reasons: as retirement sinecures, because they were ineffective classroom teachers, or because, more happily, they were genuinely interested in academic libraries. It was natural, then, that they tried to make conceptual connections between the world of books, bibliography, and libraries and the world of collegiate instruction with which they were already familiar.

Bibliographic instruction came to be viewed by some as an essential element in an undergraduate liberal arts education. One of its major spokesmen after the turn of the century was William Warner Bishop, who was, for twenty-six years, director of the library at the University of Michigan. Bishop used the term *bibliographic training* and explained what he thought should result from such instruction. Students would have the ability to judge the comparative merits of books; they would know something of the characteristics of particular authors, reviewers, and publishers. They should be able to integrate what they learned in the library with what they already knew, what they were learning in college, and what they were learning from other students. They should develop a discriminating attitude toward books (Bishop, 1912). Students needed the art of discrimination: the ability to make informed judgments on the basis of critical comparisons of authors' views and opinions. This kind of intellectual activity, defined by Newman as enlargement, was seen by Bishop as the central process of bibliographic instruction. Liberal education and bibliographic instruction would serve the same purpose: They would help create in students the ability to intelligently compare and to make critical judgments about available alternatives.

The ideals of research and their application to the solution of society's problems have contributed far less to concepts of bibliographic instruction than has liberal education. The rise of scientific historical research and the emergence of new and more specialized social science disciplines significantly stimulated the growth of bibliographic instruction but did not signal a shift in ideas about it. However, nothing less than the transformation of higher education and its purposes was under way. Major developments in the period from 1875 to 1917 included the acceptance of research on a par with teaching, the establishment of doctoral studies and other graduate programs in numerous colleges and universities, and the adoption of the seminar method of instruction (Bestor, 1953). Distinctive features of seminar teaching were the examination of a variety of sources, oral and written student presentations, and critical evaluations of student work by professors and other seminar participants.

These developments underscored the importance of bibliographic instruction but did not enhance it conceptually. Historian Herbert Baxter Adams of the Johns Hopkins University, for instance, urged librarians to plan and present lectures and courses on the bibliography of the various disciplines (Adams, 1887). At the same time, his belief that librarians should teach the ways and means of inquiry was merely suggestive rather than explanatory. The necessity of teaching graduate students to conduct research in their chosen fields found expression in the broad acceptance of required courses that introduced research methods to beginning master's and doctoral students, and such courses became a mainstay in American higher education. Generally taught by professors rather than by librarians, these courses draw their conceptual strength from the methods of inquiry unique to each discipline. Designed for graduate research and instruction, they have had little impact, historically, on concepts of bibliographic instruction as they affect undergraduates.

Similarly, the ideal of using the university to solve society's problems produced nothing new in terms of conceptual development. The establishment of land grant universities coincided with the rise of graduate research. As a consequence, the high level of energy and enthusiasm that supported the service role was quite similar in intensity to that which had fueled research. The mission of service was to offer the university's aptitude for teaching and research to the communities of agriculture and industry, among others. The critical intellectual faculties so important to the liberally educated and so essential for scholarly research in the humanities and social sciences would, henceforth, serve mechanics, farmers, artisans, and shopkeepers as well. As the president of Washington State University noted, students relied on analysis and synthesis and on observation and comparison. They, too, engaged in scientific inquiry, and they used the experimental methods and laboratory tools of the biologist, physicist, chemist, and engineer (Moos, 1982).

One author concluded that about one-third of the land grant institutions with schools of agriculture offered bibliographic instruction (Dunlap, 1925). The utilitarian nature of the academic program, nevertheless, was mirrored in the utilitarian thrust of bibliographic instruction. Nothing new emerged that would add to the modest conceptual notions already set forth.

All of these basic elements of American higher education — liberal education, research, and utility — had, by the early twentieth century, found permanent homes in the bureaucratic structures of academe and provided the environment, pedagogical methods, and intellectual stimulus for bibliographic instruction. The strength of these elements remains today and shapes concepts about the library's purposes and about its potential as a teaching instrument.

Three Periods of Bibliographic Instruction

Three distinct periods characterize the history of ideas about bibliographic instruction. The first of these, from 1870 to 1930, may be termed the era of the professor of books. This period roughly parallels the rise of graduate programs and land grant institutions as well as dramatic growth in collections and facilities for academic research libraries. The years from 1930 to 1970 constitute the library-college period and are dominated by the concepts of college teaching and library use enunciated by Louis Shores. The third period, from 1970 to the present, emerged when instruction librarians began to formulate a wide variety of theories and ideas about the nature of their work.

The conspicuous irony in the professor of books era is the inability of the small liberal arts college to alone provide the intellectual underpinnings for concepts of bibliographic instruction even though its historic purposes were firmly within the liberal arts tradition. Before the turn of the century when higher education was undergoing rapid change and growth, many institutions were forced to make new and hard decisions. Would they follow the tide, like Harvard, for example, and establish numerous doctoral programs and emphasize research as well as teaching? Or, would they remain relatively small and reemphasize their commitment to the liberal arts tradition, character development for undergraduates, and, in some cases, their denominational connections? These developments produced two distinct kinds of institutions: small private colleges with limited missions, and large private and public universities with diverse missions. The small colleges, given their regard for liberal culture, would seem more likely to formulate concepts of bibliographic instruction. However, that was not the case.

Before college librarians could fashion useful ideas about instruction, they needed models appropriate to the field of librarianship rather than the field of academic teaching. The colleges eventually found these models in the rapidly changing university libraries. Progressive leadership in the major universities was most conspiciously offered by Justin Winsor at Harvard and Raymond C. Davis at the University of Michigan, both of whose pronouncements on bibliographic teaching were highly regarded for some three or four decades thereafter (Schneider, 1912; Richardson, 1916). Winsor and Davis were joined by a chorus of university administrators who, in their attempts to find a suitable concept or metaphor for the academic library, described it as a "central and vitalizing force." President Charles W. Eliot of Harvard once exclaimed that the university could more easily accomplish its work without adequate funds than without books and adequate facilities for their use (Brough, 1953).

A concept that caught the imagination of librarians, professors, and administrators was one that emphasized centrality and the organic nature of the library and its parent institution. As the heart of the university, the library would not only be the center of the institution but also a source of energy for the intellectual needs of the academic community. This concept was a powerful tool in raising funds for libraries and thereby helping many colleges to obtain a library building specifically designed for faculty and student use.

The library as the heart of the university is a concept that served well for a passing era. By the time the emphasis on scholarship had forever stamped universities as institutions of research, this concept had fully played its role.

Consequently, another conception of the library emerged, perhaps suggested by the organizational and economic success of research in the basic sciences such as physics, chemistry, and biology. The library was seen as a laboratory for the humanities and social sciences. It provided the means for experimentation and testing and for analysis and comparison; it was as crucial to the humanist and social scientist as was the microscope or test tube to the scientist (Willard, 1897; Bishop, 1928).

These three conceptions of the academic library—as the center of the institution, as the heart of the college and university, and as the laboratory of the humanist and social scientist—coincided with the acceptance of the professor of books idea. These conceptions did not, however, lend that idea the theoretical backing sufficient to help it go much beyond Emerson's views on college education. At best, these conceptions enhanced the continuing dialogue on academic libraries, but they were only generally, rather than explicitly, suggestive of concepts about bibliographic instruction.

The years from 1930 to 1970 could rightly be called the era of the library-college. The term *library-college* may or may not have originated with Louis Shores, but Shores is generally recognized as the chief proponent of the idea. He was its most dedicated philosopher and most vocal prophet. The concept involves moving the teaching and learning situation from the classroom to the library. As envisioned by Shores in 1935, the library-college presupposed the abolition of regular class attendance in favor of studying in the library, the merging of all physical facilities into a single library complex, peer instruction of beginning undergraduates by upperclassmen, the integration of librarians and professors into a single teaching staff, and a liberal arts curriculum that focused on techniques of problem solving (Shores, 1935).

In its time, and for several decades thereafter, the library-college idea was the only clear philosophical statement of academic library service that was undergirded by accompanying objectives and that, in a theoretical sense, could support modern educational trends such as independent study and student-centered interdisciplinary learning (Breivik, 1977). The library-college is respected for its comprehensive approach to higher education and its view of the totality of learning materials as the "generic book" to which all students should be introduced. Its most compelling aspect is its thoroughgoing consistency as a concept.

On the other hand, this idea tends to be rather idealistic and unnatural. To implement its principles demands such a sweeping realignment of professional staff that it has had little impact on established institutions. As a special manifestation of the library's teaching function, it has had a substantial enough influence that it has become the subject of several retrospective critiques, among the most comprehensive and favorable of which is a doctoral dissertation at the University of Maryland (Terwilliger, 1975).

With the birth of the library-college idea, the small liberal arts college displaced the large university as the leader in forming concepts about bibliographic instruction. Although Louis Shores, at the time of his landmark article in 1935, was a library educator at George Peabody College for Teachers, he had come to that post from a small private college, Fisk University. As early as 1929, Bishop had recognized the great advantage, for instructional purposes, of the small college library over its university counterpart, due to the small library's ability to establish intimate and unrestricted relationships between books and students (Bishop, 1929). The flexibility and informality of the small college library encouraged greater experimentation and more readily enhanced service and administration in these institutions (Farber, 1974).

The present period, which begins in 1970, is the latest period in the growth of ideas about bibliographic instruction. Although we are enjoying a new, somewhat eclectic era with potentially useful concepts being suggested by a number of educators and instruction librarians, we are also witnessing what appears to be a strong trend in favor of learning theories. Jerome Bruner has argued the wisdom of teaching general principles rather than specific topics or skills. Students should be taught to generalize, to obtain knowledge that is usable beyond the immediate situation in which it was learned. Knowledge should be presented with a structure sufficient to tie it together; otherwise it constitutes only sets of unconnected, readily forgotten facts (Bruner, 1963). Basing their suggestions on Bruner's theories, Kobelski and Reichel organized the learning process into the three essential steps: acquisition (the learner's awareness of new information), assimilation (the learner relating new materials to previous knowledge), and consolidation (the learner reorganizing knowledge into new material) (Kobelski and Reichel, 1981). Ford (1979), after conducting an extensive review of the literature of cognitive psychology, proposed that the concepts of independence and structure may be central to any comprehensive theory about bibliographic instruction that might be developed in the future.

Beaubien, Hogan, and George (1982) aptly summarize the above lines of thought. Cognitive learning draws upon patterns of logic that students have already developed in order to help them understand new subject matter. By concentrating on the logical connections in this existing intellectual framework, students can add to and enhance what they already know. According to Frick (1975; 1982), bibliographic instruction is particularly adaptable to this approach, given how knowledge is organized within the disciplines and how bibliographic information is organized in libraries.

Although academic librarianship has long suffered from the absence of a theory of high informative value, meaningful progress is being made, especially in the field of bibliographic instruction. These concepts are examined by Oberman and Strauch (1982) in *Theories of Bibliographic Education*, an exploration of various concepts that the conscientious practitioner may wish to apply in succeeding decades.

Conclusion

Emerson's ideas remain amidst current development in the concepts and theories of bibliographic instruction. A significant feature of his ideas is their centrality to the notions of a liberal education that are still highly regarded by many librarians and other educators. Lindgren (1978), for example, considers that bibliographic instruction must include an examination of the premises underlying logical analysis and must inculcate in students the ability to exert critical judgments and to use the library as a resource. Thus, the aspect of comparison and the art of discrimination are considered as necessary today as they were in the nineteenth century.

Not surprisingly, a theme in recent concepts of bibliographic instruction is the idea of independence. Students should, after appropriate instruction, be able to teach themselves and to rely on the underlying logic of library and bibliographic knowledge and on their own ability to analyze information in direct relation to their research needs. This independence, with its high regard for the learner, is distinctly Emerson. The importance of independence in library research is underscored by the fact that the structure of knowledge in the subject disciplines and in bibliographic systems is becoming increasingly complex. The instruction librarian who would turn dependent researchers into independent ones faces a task that is difficult but ultimately manageable.

References

Adams, H. B. "Seminary Libraries and University Extension." *Johns Hopkins University Studies in Historical and Political Science,* 1887, *5* (11), 443–459.

Beaubien, A. K., Hogan, S. A., and George, M. W. *Learning the Library: Concepts and Methods for Effective Bibliographic Instruction.* New York: Bowker, 1982.

Bestor, A. E., Jr. "The Transformation of American Scholarship, 1875–1917." *Library Quarterly,* 1953, *23* (3), 164–179.

Bisbee, M. D. "The Place of Bibliography in the Equipment of an Educated Man." *Library Journal,* 1897, *22* (9), 429–432.

Bishop, W. W. "Training in the Use of Books." *Sewanee Review,* 1912, *20* (3), 265–281.

Bishop, W. W. "The Contribution of the Library to College Teaching." *Association of American Colleges Bulletin,* 1928, *14* (5), 437–441.

Bishop, W. W. "The Library in the American College." In ACRL (Ed.), *College and Reference Library Yearbook.* Chicago: American Library Association, 1929.

Breivik, P. S. *Open Admissions and the Academic Library.* Chicago: American Library Association, 1977.

Broadus, R. N. "Library Science and Liberal Education." *Journal of Education for Librarianship,* 1967, *1* (4), 203–209.

Brough, K. J. *Scholar's Workshop: Evolving Conceptions of Library Service.* Urbana: University of Illinois Press, 1953.

Brubacher, J. S. *On the Philosophy of Higher Education.* San Francisco: Jossey-Bass, 1977.

Bruner, J. S. *The Process of Education.* Cambridge, Mass.: Harvard University Press, 1963.

Davis, R. C. "Teaching Bibliography in Colleges." *Library Journal,* 1886, *11* (8–9), 289–294.

Dunlap, F. "Training the Agricultural Freshman to Use the Library." *Public Libraries,* 1925, *30* (7), 394–395.

Emerson, R. W. "Books." *Atlantic Monthly,* 1858, *1* (3), 343–353.

Farber, E. I. "College Librarians and the University-Library Syndrome." In E. I. Farber and R. Walling (Eds.), *The Academic Library: Essays in Honor of Guy R. Lyle.* Metuchen, N.J.: Scarecrow Press, 1974.

Ford, N. "Cognitive Psychology and 'Library Learning.'" *Journal of Librarianship,* 1979, *11* (1), 25–38.

Frick, E. "Information Structure and Bibliographic Instruction." *Journal of Academic Librarianship,* 1975, *1* (4), 12–14.

Frick, E. "Teaching Information Structure: Turning Dependent Researchers into Self-Teachers." In C. Oberman and K. Strauch (Eds.), *Theories of Bibliographic Education: Designs for Teaching.* New York: Bowker, 1982.

Knapp, P. B. *The Monteith College Library Experiment.* New York: Scarecrow Press, 1966.

Kobelski, P., and Reichel, M. "Conceptual Frameworks for Bibliographic Instruction." *Journal of Academic Librarianship,* 1981, *7* (2), 73–77.

Lindgren, J. "Seeking a Useful Tradition for Library User Instruction in College Library." In J. Lubans, Jr. (Ed.), *Progress in Educating the Library User.* New York: Bowker, 1978.

Little, G. T. "School and College Libraries." *Library Journal,* 1893, *18* (10), 431–433.

McMullen, H. "Ralph Waldo Emerson and Libraries." *Library Quarterly,* 1955, *25* (2), 152–162.

Maddock, L. N. "Emerson on Education." *Educational Theory,* 1957, *7* (1), 56–58.

Moos, M. "The Future of the Land Grant University." *Change,* 1982, *14* (3), 30–35.

Newman, J. H. *The Idea of a University.* Garden City, N.Y.: Doubleday, 1959. (Originally published in 1853.)

Oberlin College. *Oberlin College Catalogue, 1903.* Oberlin, Ohio: Oberlin College, 1903.

Oberman, C., and Strauch, K. (Eds.). *Theories of Bibliographic Education: Designs for Teaching.* New York: Bowker, 1982.

Perkins, F. B. "On Professorships of Books and Reading." In U.S. Bureau of Education (Ed.), *Public Libraries in the United States of America: Their History, Condition, and Management.* Washington, D.C.: U.S. Government Printing Office, 1876.

Poole, W. F. "The University Library and the University Curriculum." *Library Journal,* 1893, *18* (11), 470–471.

Richardson, E. C. "Extracts from a Paper on the Place of the Library in a University." In A. S. Root (Ed.), *American Library Institute Papers and Proceedings.* Chicago: American Library Association, 1916.

Schneider, J. "A College Course in Bibliography." *Catholic Educational Review,* 1912, *3* (3), 215–222.

Shaw, C. B. "Bibliographical Instructions for Students." *Library Journal,* 1928, *53* (7), 300–301.

Shores, L. "The Library Arts College, a Possibility in 1954?" *School and Society,* 1935, *41* (1048), 110–114.

Shores, L. "The College of Library Art, 1984." *Journal of Education for Librarianship,* 1964, *4* (3), 125–136.

Terwilliger, G. H. P. "The Library-College: A Movement for Experimental and Innovative Learning Concepts: Applications and Implications for Higher Education." Unpublished doctoral dissertation, University of Maryland, 1975.

Tucker, J. M. "The Liberal Arts Foundation of Library Use Instruction." *Indiana Libraries,* 1981, *1* (1), 19–25.

Veysey, L. R. *The Emergence of the American University.* Chicago: University of Chicago Press, 1965.

Wayman, V. "A Study of Emerson's Philosophy of Education." *Education,* 1936, *56* (8), 474–482.

Willard, A. R. "College Libraries in the United States." *New England Magazine,* 1897, *17* (4), 422–440.

John Mark Tucker is senior reference librarian and assistant professor of library science at Purdue University. He presently is a doctoral candidate at the University of Illinois and was reference librarian at Wabash College from 1973 to 1979.

*Library use instruction, when viewed as a discipline,
encourages the development of patterns of critical thought
in the independent inquirer.*

Library Use
and the Development
of Critical Thought

Stephen H. Plum

Library instruction should develop in the student those patterns of critical thought that lead to efficient and independent library inquiry. These patterns of thought enable the student to interact successfully with the information systems of an academic library and thus to identify and locate the information relevant to the student's problem or question. The interaction of the student with library systems shares characteristics with the process of problem solving, and instruction in library use increases the possibility of productive interaction. Of great interest to bibliographic instruction librarians is the nature of student patterns of thought. On what habits of thought can the student draw that lead to the creative and systematic discovery of information? What kinds of teaching instill the desired patterns of thought? What structure or framework supports bibliographic instruction?

The most useful framework is provided by the context of the discipline area of study; that is, the process of original research in a discipline and the use of a discipline's literature and its library information systems. Discipline context provides structure to library use instruction and develops the desired patterns of thought in the independent inquirer. The following experiences in teaching two upper-level, bibliographic instruction courses support the importance of the role of the discipline context in library use instruction. The dis-

T. G. Kirk (Ed.). *Increasing the Teaching Role of Academic Libraries.*
New Directions for Teaching and Learning, no. 18. San Francisco: Jossey-Bass, June 1984.

cussion below draws examples from a bibliographic instruction course for research in English and American literature and contrasts these examples with the lesson of an analogous course in literature research in science.

Discipline Context as Structure

The need for structure in bibliographic instruction has been noted by Smalley (1977), Lindgren (1978), and Kobelski and Reichel (1981). Although a variety of frameworks have been offered, Knapp (1966) and Frick (1982), among others, have advocated that the nature of scholarly research within a discipline provides the desired structure or framework. Some have recommended the next logical step as well. If the nature of the discipline somehow informs learning in bibliographic instruction, then, as McInnis (1978), Hopkins (1981), Keresztesi (1982), and Beaubien and others (1982) suggest, relationships between epistemological concerns of the discipline and the points at which the concerns manifest themselves in published literature and in the library information systems must be subjected to systematic study by bibliographic instruction or reference librarians.

Discipline context as presented here consists of three elements: the process of original research within the discipline; the structure of the literature that flows from, and is itself a part of, that research; and the library information systems developed to identify information within that literature. Relying heavily on some of the principles outlined in Smalley and Plum (1982), this discussion explores the possibilities inherent in this framework for library use instruction.

Within the process of original research converge the research methodology, the objects of study, and the epistemological features of the discipline that make it different from all other disciplines. What are the approaches to knowledge that make research in a particular discipline distinctive? In the study of literary works, for example, it may be proposed that research is the unique encounter of the personal interpretation of the research with the written product of human creativity, the text. Literary criticism builds on the contributions of textual criticism, historical scholarship, and linguistics. Although centered in the individual work, it searches for relationships between the work and the total body of writing produced by the author, genre, convention, or literary history (Frye, 1970). Creativivy lies in exploring previously unseen or unexpressed relationships.

Research methods, or the principles behind criticism, are not universally accepted within the discipline. A variety of critical approaches to a single work can legitimately arrive at different, yet valid, interpretations and criticisms. Personal interaction plays an important role, and criticism by scholars stemming from a common critical approach can also differ. Thus, current research in the study of literature tends not to supercede older work, just as the literature of the twentieth century does not replace earlier literature. In certain tasks of literary scholarship, such as in the establishment of texts, knowledge apparently does accumulate, but in most other activities it does not.

The process of original research results in a published document. Without publication the research is not complete, for only then is knowledge communicated to the profession. What are the physical characteristics of the literature; that is, in what form of publication does the literature usually appear? What type of information is generally acceptable? How does the review process take place? The answers to these and other questions form the second aspect of the discipline context — the structure of the literature.

Scholarly work in the study of literature often requires thorough explanation of the critical principles or methods used in the analysis. The relationships that original research explores between the work and the concerns mentioned by Frye encourage careful argumentation. Because of the personal element involved in interpretation, the critic's own thought process and reasons for belief become matters of interest in addition to the critical treatment of a text. Furthermore, the noncumulative character of knowledge permits the researcher time to reflect and to investigate problems with little likelihood that another researcher will examine the same relationships in precisely the same way. Therefore, the monograph is the predominant vehicle for scholarly communication, and, as a consequence, book reviews are the primary mechanism for peer evaluation.

Systems of informational access in the library share with the literature they identify, and with the research process that produces the literature, some of the distinctive characteristics of the discipline. Not only does the structure of relatively esoteric reference tools mirror the disciplinary nature of their subject, but even a tool as prosaic as the card catalogue reflects a distinctive discipline orientation.

In the card catalogue, for example, the Library of Congress subject headings assigned to monographs in literary scholarship correspond to the interest in relationships between the text and the other constructs noted in the research process. Subject headings provide access by personal name, the personal name accompanied by the name of the work, the time period in which the author published, the name of the movement (if any) with which the author is identified, the national tradition, and the genre or type of work. The Library of Congress classification system (which is a system for organizing books on the shelves) reflects the author's chronological place within a national tradition and facilitates browsing the literary researchers.

If one accepts the discipline context of bibliographic information, this does not necessarily imply that the structure of bibliographic instruction courses must follow an identical organization. The structure of the conceptual framework does not necessarily determine the structure of the course, although it may guide the instructor's choices. However, any method of teaching that grows from an understanding of the discipline context would aid in developing the desired patterns of thought in the student.

Erroneous Conceptual Frameworks

Productive conceptual frameworks encourage meaningful learning and the transfer of learning to new situations and help develop patterns of critical thought that make students effective independent inquirers in the library. Erroneous conceptual frameworks are nonproductive in the creation of such learning patterns. Four such nonproductive conceptual frameworks are concerned with: (1) motivation of the learner, (2) theories of learning, (3) the mechanical structure of courses, and (4) particular reference tools used.

For bibliographic instruction courses, motivation can serve as an adjunct to conceptual structure, but it is not a substitute for it. Similarly, learning theory is often used by teachers to formulate teaching approaches, but it does not by itself provide conceptual structure for bibliographic instruction. Mechanical structure, the way the course is taught, may also not, in itself, constitute a conceptual structure that leads to the development of independent researching skills in students. The mechanical structure and method of teaching should be chosen with an awareness of the conceptual structure of the course, and should not simply be based on logistical considerations.

Specific reference tools or types of reference tools also do not constitute conceptual framework. Both the arrangement and scope of a particular reference tool and its purpose are influenced by the discipline context. To teach a course in the use of a type of reference tool, such as bibliographies, without consideration of the discipline context is to employ a type-of-tool approach to bibliographic instruction. The type-of-tool method has been derogated as the library science approach; this seems to be the most telling criticism about an often thoroughly unpopular course. As the amount of information increases, the number and complexity of reference tools also dramatically increases (Murray, 1981). Keresztesi (1982), points out that the proliferation of reference tools makes the item-by-item survey increasingly unwieldly. Many reference tools are being offered on-line, on microfilm, or in other nontraditional modes of access. Keresztesi also argues that an ordered bibliographic universe is necessary to make the world of scholarly disciplines intelligible to library users. The order is found in the discipline not in a list of reference tools.

Patterns of Critical Thought

With instruction, students can learn to find evidence relevant to their topic, understand the use of citations and the purposes of documentation, and use intricately arranged reference tools well. Students taught to be systematic and logical in their information inquiry should then, having found possible sources of information, be able to evaluate them quickly and accurately.

Topic Selection and the Nature of Evidence. Lindgren (1982) considers the process of topic selection and the associated focusing process similar to collecting evidence to support an argument. Knapp (1966) observes that, when looking for information, students tend to seek answers to questions rather than attempting to find evidence to support a thesis. Research questions that appear to be merely answerable may be simple fact or background reference questions. Topic statements that attempt to encompass too many ideas or that are undefinable may be unresearchable due to lack of appropriate evidence. There is no easy way to distinguish inappropriate evidence from what is constructive.

The student can independently and confidently engage in topic selection and the determination of suitable evidence when both are related to discipline context. Not only is the subject matter of topics distinctive but questions of what constitutes an appropriate topic or relevant evidence are also distinctive for each discipline. For example, scholarly literary work arises from the interplay between the content and meaning of the topic and the researcher's interpretation and involvement. This interaction can be displayed by assigning a designated work by an author as the focus of bibliographic research and then requiring that the student develop a thesis statement from a personal perspective with sufficient scope to result in a ten-page paper. By contrast, a course in literature searching in a scientific field would assign students very specific and explicit research topics, since, within paradigmatic frameworks, knowledge in the sciences is generally cumulative and guided by theory. Literature searching in the sciences verifies whether or not the problem under investigation has already been resolved, and whether it is capable of being solved within theoretical limitations.

The nature of expected and acceptable evidence can be analyzed on several discipline-determined levels. The ways of thought unique to a discipline, its epistemological models, and its process of research constitute one level of analysis. Subject content — not only relevance but also the appropriateness of the subject to the discipline — is another level. The structural features of a discipline's literature are a third level. The form of publication (monographs), the type of information (statistical data), and the nature of primary and secondary materials and their anticipated mix are all parts of the discipline context that reflect the structure of the literature.

The student who is attentive to the discipline context knows how to approach topic selection and determine appropriate, acceptable evidence and avoids the pitfalls of looking for unsuitable evidence to support an unresearchable topic.

Documentation and the Use of Citations. Associated with the idea of evidence is the process of documentation. A course in bibliographic instruction should teach students a standard format for citations as well as the reasons for citing. Style manuals that specify standard formats for citations are often associated with specific disciplines. The reasons for and the uses of references vary widely among different areas of study. As Smalley and Plum (1982) point out, documentation in literary research enables the reader to identify sources and gives authority and credibility to the work. When to cite involves value judgment, and the use of citations can strengthen or disrupt an argument. Students should be encouraged to use citations creatively, even artistically. To teach judgment in literary research, students should be required to write selective, but not exhaustive, bibliographies.

In the sciences, the purpose of citation is to demonstrate that the relevant literature has been thoroughly investigated, to show that the current research effort is new and necessary, to document that the proposed research builds on that which has preceded it, and to enable others to identify the cited reports. Therefore, citation use in the sciences is systematic.

Understanding citation format reduces the need to return to the literature to verify incomplete references. Understanding reasons behind documentation guides the student in the search, for it gives a view of the end result to which the literature search is the means.

Structure of Reference Tools. Each discipline has unique reference tools that integrate and provide access to information, but how does the nature of knowledge within a discipline influence the structure, arrangement, scope, and purpose of its reference tools? An appreciation of why certain reference tools are structured in particular ways helps students understand that a tool is internally accessible and that it will be of help.

Research in English and American literature explores relationships between an artist's work and an artist, the genre, the characteristics of the time period, the national tradition, and other similar questions. The structure of literary reference works reflect these approaches. For example, the pre-1981 *MLA International Bibliography* is arranged by national literatures, chronologically subdivided, and subsequently indexed by the name of the author whose work is the subject of the reference. In the case of an author whose critical treatment is voluminous, (for example, Shakespeare) it is further divided by the names of individual titles. The student who understands the customary interrelationships in literary criticism is able to use the tool more successfully than the student who does not.

The importance of the critic's interpretative framework and experience in literary research carries over to the construction of reference tools. The author of the reference tool attempts to encourage the interaction of the reader with the subject matter by arranging the tool in ways that emphasize certain relationships. Therefore, reference tools in literary research may cover the same subject matter, be equally contributive, and not be repetitive. The student who appreciates this phenomenon can search more successfully.

Evaluation of Sources. In each scholarly discipline, researchers constantly evaluate published material. The criteria against which the worth of the publication is judged and the mechanism by which the evaluation occurs are discipline determined. Literary criticism is itself the test of value for the applications of textual, linguistic, and historical studies in the study of literature (Lipking, 1981). Accusations of faulty scholarship can therefore rest on the evidence of the text that is being examined. Criticism must also adhere to correct reasoning and logic. While these two standards are easier to apply, Lipking points to two other standards that cause more difficulty in literary criticism. Because not only knowledge but ways of knowing are within the purview of scholarship in literary research, the principles of criticism can be criticized. So, too, can the interpretive validity of the contribution be judged either authentic or inauthentic. The last standard is based on the critic's personal interpretation of the text.

Because of the predominance of the monograph, the primary mechanism of evaluation in literary research is the book review. Judgments on critical method or on interpretive validity are often debatable, so the author of the book is usually offered a forum for response.

Although the quantity of accessible information has dramatically multiplied, the amount of time available to the student or researcher to assimilate the information has not. Therefore, selection and evaluation of sources assumes an increasingly important role in the search for information and in bibliographic instruction.

Research Strategy. In Rogers' (1980) treatment of research strategy, the term *strategy* is loosely defined as the systematic approach to information. Rogers discusses efforts to place the process of information searching within the substantive and bibliographic structures of disciplines, particularly those made by McInnis (1978). The resulting research strategies lead to self-sufficient inquiry, efficient use of time, exhaustive or precise information gathering (depending on the need), and the retrieval of the most appropriate sources.

In bibliographic instruction in English and American literature, open and creative research strategies should be encouraged that reflect the methodological freedom found in the discipline. By making the student aware of the search as a process, by suggesting alternative routes or strategies to information, and by encouraging receptivity and curiosity in the student when confronted with unfamiliar reference tools, patterns of creative searching can be instilled.

Bibliographic instruction in a scientific field would likewise focus on student development of approaches to the search process that correspond to ways of understanding in the discipline. Systematic testing of the research problem against the literature, in a manner analogous to the testing of a hypothesis against the natural world, would be presented as the normal or correct method.

Research strategy is also influenced by a discipline's distinctive mechanism of evaluation. In the sciences, for example, one search strategy that exploits the evaluative mechanism and its citation patterns has the student begin with an annual review article and identify the important articles pertaining to the research problem. Information conveyed by these articles is then updated and evaluated by using the *Science Citation Index.* In literary scholarship, a selective author bibliography could be the beginning of systematic inquiry that builds on, teaches, and illuminates the process of evaluation in that discipline.

Conclusion

Distinctive processes of original research, literature structures, and library systems that organize and identify that literature comprise particular discipline contexts. These function in important ways to influence patterns of thought in the independent library researcher. Bibliographic instruction that uses discipline context as conceptual framework fosters the growth of attitudes that mark the independent and critical inquirer.

An interesting question, however, can be raised as to whether this approach can be applied to bibliographic instruction courses required of all students by general education programs. It cannot, according to Freides (1983), but she is skeptical about the usefulness of the discipline context in any bibliographic instruction course. Students in required general education courses are usually freshmen or sophomores and may not have developed awareness of the distinctive logic that characterizes an area of study.

If the discipline context is a valid concept, it ought to provide a useful structure for this type of course and for the process of learning for students. The popularity of general education programs and the substantial number of such programs incorporating library use instruction components raise exciting possibilities for growth and learning, both for students and for the librarians who must respond to the challenge of devising courses that produce independent and competent researchers.

References

Beaubien, A. K., Hogan, S. A., and George, M. W. *Learning the Library: Concepts and Methods for Effective Bibliographic Instruction.* New York: Bowker, 1982.

Freides, T. "Current Trends in Academic Libraries." *Library Trends,* 1983, *31* (3), 457–474.

Frick, E. "Teaching Information Structure: Turning Dependent Researchers into Self-Teachers." In C. Oberman and K. Strauch (Eds.), *Theories of Bibliographic Education: Designs for Teaching.* New York: Bowker, 1982.

Frye, N. "Literary Criticism." In J. Thorpe (Ed.), *The Aims and Methods of Scholarship in Modern Languages and Literatures.* 2nd ed. New York: Modern Language Association of America, 1970.

Hopkins, F. L. "Bibliographic Instruction: An Emerging Professional Discipline." In C.A. Kirkendall (Ed.), *Directions for the Decade: Library Instruction in the 1980s.* Ann Arbor, Mich.: Pierian Press, 1981.

Keresztesi, M. "The Science of Bibliography: Theoretical Implications of Bibliographic Instruction." In C. Oberman and K. Strauch (Eds.), *Theories of Bibliographic Education: Designs for Teaching.* New York: Bowker, 1982.

Knapp, P. B. *The Monteith College Library Experiment.* New York: Scarecrow Press, 1966.

Kobelski, P., and Reichel, M. "Conceptual Frameworks for Bibliographic Instruction." *Journal of Academic Librarianship,* 1981, *7* (2), 73–77.

Lindgren, J. "Seeking a Useful Tradition for Library User Instruction in the College Library." In J. Lubans (Ed.), *Progress in Educating the Library User.* New York: Bowker, 1978.

Lindgren, J. "The Idea of Evidence in Bibliographic Inquiry." In C. Oberman and K. Strauch (Eds.), *Theories of Bibliographic Education: Designs for Teaching.* New York: Bowker, 1982.

Lipking, L. "Literary Criticism." In J. Gilbaldi (Ed.), *Introduction to Scholarship in Modern Languages and Literatures.* New York: Modern Language Association of America, 1981.

McInnis, R. G. *New Perspectives for Reference Service in Academic Libraries.* Westport, Conn.: Greenwood, 1978.

Murray, K. "Advances in Reference Services." In M. H. Harris (Ed.), *Advances in Librarianship,* vol. 11. New York: Academic, 1981.

Rogers, S. J. "Research Strategies: Bibliographic Instruction for Undergraduates." *Library Trends,* 1980, *29* (1), 69–82.

Smalley, T. N. "Bibliographic Instruction in Academic Libraries: Questioning Some Assumptions." *Journal of Academic Librarianship,* 1977, *3* (5), 280–283.

Smalley, T. N., and Plum, S. H. "Teaching Library Researching in the Humanities and the Sciences: A Contextual Approach." In C. Oberman and K. Strauch (Eds.), *Theories of Bibliographic Education: Designs for Teaching.* New York: Bowker, 1982.

Stephen H. Plum is senior assistant librarian for reference at State University of New York College at Plattsburgh.

A basic element of bibliographic instruction is the teaching of search strategy.

Patterns for Research

Cerise Oberman

Assignment. Write a fifteen-page research paper on women and the military. Support your paper with at least one book and five periodical articles.

Scenario

Bob begins by going to the library with a list of sources provided by the instructor. He uses a general encyclopedia to gather background information but finds that frustrating—there is nothing on his topic. He then searches in the card catalogue for possible book titles. He has a difficult time locating books on the topic although he uses the standardized vocabulary for card catalogue subject headings. He finally locates one book and decides that it will satisfy the assignment. He uses *Readers' Guide to Periodical Literature* for locating periodical articles and finds a number of articles. He selects those from *Newsweek, Time, People, Ms,* and *U.S. News and World Report.* Bob's research is completed.

Scenario

Alice begins by examining the assigned topic. On what aspect of women and the military will she concentrate? She considers several options: women in combat, women in the Navy, women as officers. After narrowing the assignment, she matches her topic with possible reference sources. She dis-

T. G. Kirk (Ed.). *Increasing the Teaching Role of Academic Libraries.*
New Directions for Teaching and Learning, no. 18. San Francisco: Jossey-Bass, June 1984.

cards encyclopedias since the topic is too recent, makes a list of possible subject headings under which information can be located, and selects the possible indexes from which she can locate primary as well as secondary sources. Only after completing this preresearch process does she go to the library. There, Alice locates several books on her topic, examines each book, and consults book reviews. To ensure a balance of scholarly and popular materials, she uses *Readers' Guide to Periodical Literature, Public Affairs Information Service, United States Monthly Catalog,* and the *New York Times Index.* He literature search results in articles from *Nation, Ms, New York Times, Military Law Review,* and a Congressional report. Alice carefully examines her research materials and finds that she has been successful in finding evidence to support her working thesis.

These scenes depict what might be typical student research behavior. While Alice's approach may be the ideal, Bob's approach, unfortunately, is more common. There is, obviously, both a substantive and qualitative difference between these two approaches. Bob, one might say, is tool-wise, but concept-weak. He has learned that research follows a prescribed pattern which usually begins with the gathering of background information, using encyclopedias, and progresses to the assembling of periodical articles, using periodical indexes. He understands these basic and fundamental concepts of information access, but his entire pattern of research is limited by the degree of his awareness and skill in using tools.

Alice's behavior, on the other hand, is more complex. While she too understands the use of tools, she also understands and applies additional research concepts. These concepts aid her in focusing and defining her topic and selecting and judging appropriate materials. Her ability to apply these concepts allows her to be more systematic, analytical, and thorough in her research.

Search Strategy

The use of search strategy as a conceptual framework or organizational scheme for teaching students research techniques has dominated library instruction for the last decade, and for good reason. It has been a simple and adaptable teaching framework. Although the term *search strategy* has been used to define various systems of ordering research (Rogers, 1980), it can be generalized: "Search strategy... is the organization of the various types of fact-finding and hybrid tools in a logical, efficient order to solve a given research problem. Once the tools have been ordered according to type, it is relatively simple to determine the most appropriate title or specific tools of each type to be consulted at each point" (Beaubien and others, 1982, p. 89). Thus, the focus of search strategy instruction is on the progression of gathering information through the use of tools. The usual progression moves from gathering background information — using encyclopedias — to locating specific articles — using indexes or abstracting tools. According to the nature of the research subject, other tools such as handbooks, atlases, book reviews, and so on are often included as part of the progression. Furthermore, the selection of tools depends on the level of the students. For instance, upper-division or graduate students should use more sophisticated and complex tools than lower-division students. Search strategy theory is a mechanical process which depends on tools to provide the framework for research.

The search strategy framework was a pioneering concept in introducing students to libraries, research, and tools. While its shortcomings are now frequently cited as reasons for abandoning or modifying it (Frick, 1975; MacGregor and McInnis, 1977; Smalley, 1977), the concept of search strategy should not be overlooked. Though search strategy is generally taught as a tool-based process, it suggests three important concepts: (1) recognition of distinct types of tools (encyclopedias, bibliographies, indexes, handbooks, and so on), (2) recognition of different source materials (books, articles, maps, and so on), and (3) recognition of a basic research pattern (from general to specific). These concepts, at the very least, should be reflected in the research process.

It would be misleading to suggest that all library instruction has centered solely on the search strategy model. This is not the case. In recent years, in particular, other conceptual frameworks have emerged. Kobelski and Reichel have examined a number of these other frameworks, including citation patterns, forms of publication, primary and secondary sources, publication sequence, and index structure among others (Kobelski and Reichel, 1981). Of existing models for teaching (regardless of formats such as workbooks, computer-assisted instruction, lecture, and so on), it is the search strategy framework, not surprisingly, which remains the most widely used.

There is, then, an important reasons for seeking new concepts for library instruction. While the search strategy model as described here has been an effective means of instruction, it ultimately misrepresents the complex nature of research by simplifying the process. Patterns of research differ for every subject topic; research is not generic. The concepts presented by Kobelski and Reichel, some of which are now gaining prominence in library instruction, transcend the simplistic process-tool approach. Indeed, they complement and expand on the search strategy model. They address the need for students in the larger context of knowledge definition, production, arrangement, and evaluation.

Students need to be taught patterns of research and the means to formulate a search strategy specifically for their individual research needs. A step toward a new and dynamic search strategy model can be taken by incorporating three research concepts — question analysis, discipline growth and scholarly communication patterns, and evaluation — with a sense of the progression of research.

Question Analysis

Before any research can begin, the topic of research must be clearly defined. This sounds simple. Yet the vast majority of students neither recognize the value nor understand the process of this preresearch step. Reference librarians are acutely attuned to this problem. Faced on a daily basis with students seeking assistance in locating material for broad, open-ended research topics, the reference librarian often takes the student through an oral rendition of question analysis. Question analysis must be the first stage of research.

Question analysis, or research problem analysis (Beaubien and others, 1982), is the process of analyzing the components of a question. This analysis achieves three important research functions: (1) it defines and focuses the topic, (2) it assists in identifying types of materials necessary for research, and (3) it introduces the relationship between fields of study and tools.

Identifying the scope of a research topic is the beginning of question analysis. One model of question analysis identifies four distinct variables to consider in defining scope: the time period that the topic covers; the geographic coverage of the topic; the interest group on which the topic will focus; and the implication or component of the topic, for instance, economic, political, sociological, psychological (Oberman, 1983). Certainly these are not the only variables that define the scope (Beaubien and others, 1982). They do, however, suggest the method of restriction.

Once the research question is defined, identifying pertinent fields of study or disciplines is the second aspect of directing research. Discipline identification is an essential element in question analysis. Reference tools are usually created for specific disciplines, which makes the interrelationship of disciplines and reference tools significant. Understanding this relationship allows for proper selection of reference materials. Additionally, discipline identification plays an important role in understanding patterns of scholarly communication.

Part of question analysis concentrates on identifying types of sources that need to be located. For teaching on an undergraduate level, this means a discussion of basic material formats—books, periodicals, government publications, annual reports, and so on. At a more advanced level, the discussion concentrates on distinguishing primary and secondary materials and their respective research uses. By identifying formats of materials necessary for research, access patterns are more easily established.

Question analysis, as a research concept, constitutes a pattern for research to follow: focus, format, find. Unlike traditional search strategy, it underscores the differences, rather than the similarities, between research needs.

Let us examine the impact of question analysis, or its lack, on Bob's and Alice's respective search methodologies. While both Bob and Alice locate information on their subjects, Bob's general approach to the topic of women in the military was random. While he understood and followed the general patterns of research, he failed to produce a focused, well-rounded paper because he has failed to identify a particular issue. Likewise, he failed to select the most appropriate intermediary tools because he did not identify appropriate disciplines. Finally, he failed to include a range of sources because he did not consider the types of information he needed.

Alice, on the other hand, carefully applied question analysis to her topic. As a result, she identified a specific issue to be explored, such as the present controversy surrounding the use of United States Army enlisted women in combat. She identified possible sources of information: books, magazines, journals, newspapers, government reports, Congressional hearings. She also identified disciplines that encompass her topic—history, political science, women's studies, sociology. By formulating a pattern for research before actually beginning, Alice is more likely to produce a focused paper.

Creation and Use of Information

Speaking at a recent conference on the future of library instruction, Fran Hopkins (1981) suggested that, "In order to use library resources effectively, students need to connect them with a basic understanding of how knowledge differs structurally from one field to another, and how bibliographic sources reflect the various stages of a knowledge process" (p. 18). Hopkins is referring to a crucial, and, until recently, missing concept in teaching students research. She is speaking of the need for students to understand: (1) the connection between the development and growth of a discipline and the information that the discipline generates, and (2) the distinct characteristics, types of sources, and use of those sources that distinguish one field of study from another. Through an understanding and awareness of these separate but interconnected concepts, the research process becomes a dynamic rather than a static process.

Discipline Development. Michael Keresztesi, a leading theorist in the concept of discipline and bibliographic development, suggests that all disciplines, in both the sciences and humanities, share certain developmental characteristics. These traits, events in the discipline's growth and its intrinsic bibliographic chain, can be generalized into three stages. The first is the pioneering stage: the discipline struggles for attention, recognition, and converts. During this phase, the bibliographic chain is characterized by informal communications—newsletters, bulletins, papers at conferences, polemical writings, and so on. The second stage of development is elaboration and proliferation: the discipline struggles for scientific legitimacy and acceptance. The bibliographic chain becomes more standardized and may include such items as biographical directories, yearbooks, official journals, textbooks, guides to the

40

subject literature, separate indexing and abstracting services, subject dictionaries, annual reviews, and subject encyclopedias. The final stage, the establishment stage, signifies the discipline's achievement of academic respectability. At this level the bibliographic chain includes highly specialized publications, listings of research consultants, and establishment of research centers and institutes (Keresztesi, 1982).

When students understand this growth pattern, it provides them with a "framework that both describes the generation of knowledge in a field and simultaneously allows them to anticipate the problematic bibliographic control of that knowledge" (Beaubien and others, 1982, p. 96). Using this model and concept of information generation and control, the researcher has a pattern with which to understand the stimulus for information production and the parallel development of a discipline and bibliographic chain.

Research Patterns. Although Keresztesi's model is useful to examine and identify the concept of information maturation, understanding how the bibliographic chain is used with specific disciplines is equally important. Information generation exists within the context of a discipline. Understanding differences in information importance and scholarly communication patterns between the humanities and sciences increases the researcher's ability to effectively access and use information. The researcher must understand the research methodologies, the nature of communication, and the products of scholarly communication (Smalley and Plum, 1982; McInnis, 1978).

Research and communication patterns in the humanities and the sciences differ significantly. Differences are manifest in both the structure of the literature and the research process. For instance, research in the humanities is generally done individually; scientific research is characteristically group work. Use of retrospective as well as current material is essential in the humanities; currency of information is emphasized almost exclusively in the sciences. Monographs, journal literature, and archival materials are the crucial elements in the humanities; science relies almost entirely on journal literature, proceedings, and the "invisible college" (Smalley and Plum, 1982; Garfield, 1980).

Returning to the opening scenarios, let us see how Alice would apply the concepts of discipline development and disciplinary research patterns. Alice knows that her topic encompasses information which may be found in history, political science, and women's studies. She recognizes that history and political science are "established" fields and that access to information will be well established. However, women's studies is a comparatively new field; Alice is aware that the bibliographic chain may not be fully developed. This will temper her expectations regarding bibliographic control of this material. Alice also understands that her topic falls within the domain of both the social sciences and humanities. Thus, she is sensitive to the use of retrospective materials, even though her topic will probably force her to rely heavily on current materials.

Judgment and Evaluation

Quantity of information is something we rarely lack. Ironically, it is the existence of so much information that is the root of a serious problem: how to evaluate and select the best information. Students are rarely equipped with either the background or the knowledge to effectively evaluate, compare, and select material based solely on its authorship or research quality. As a result, most students find vast quantities of materials, but their selection of material is generally random. It is the ability to "distinguish between appropriate, and inappropriate, scholarly and popular material. . . [that] is a mandatory talent for college students" (Frick, 1982, p. 197). An understanding of these differences is crucial to successful student research.

Traditionally, the evaluation of book-length materials is introduced through book review indexes. Knowing about book reviews, however, is not enough. The proliferation of book reviews of all types, lengths, and quality often only adds to the confusion. It is far more important to learn how to evaluate the quality of a book review. For instance, student researchers must be taught to recognize the reviewer's credentials, as reflected in his or her inclusion of a thorough explication of the book's thesis, examination of the book's strengths and weaknesses, and comparison of the importance of the book to others in its field. Learning to understand the perspectives and biases of reviewers reinforces the value of the evaluation process.

Evaluating other types of materials (articles, reports, and so forth) is more difficult since they are not subject to systematic evaluation by peers. Therefore, the weight of evaluation falls to the researcher. Providing a basis for evaluation requires first teaching the differences between popular and scholarly periodicals. The differences between periodicals can be judged using a set of criteria that assist in recognizing and categorizing the difference in information quality. This set of criteria can include authorship, audience, format, and breadth and depth of information.

Discovering and tracing fundamental sources (key sources) is another evaluation and judgment framework. Key sources are those sources which provide the conceptual focus or direction of inquiry for a particular area of study (McInnis, 1978). Key sources play an integral role in at least one theory of research strategy (McInnis, 1978), and they also offer a mechanism for evaluation.

The recurrence of a citation in bibliographies, encyclopedias, handbooks, literature reviews, and so on alerts the researcher to the importance of that particular work. By using citation indexes, researchers can trace the relationship between the cited document and the citing document. While there are multiple reasons for a work to be cited, it is not uncommon for citing material to present subsequent supportive or argumentative literature on the original key source (Smith, 1981).

Understanding key sources and citation patterns provides a framework for: (1) recognizing and isolating standard research in a field, (2) tracing subsequent related research, and (3) acknowledging the judgment and evaluation that researchers bring to a key source. Ultimately, this allows for a more informed and knowledgeable evaluation and selection of material.

The importance of judgment and evaluation are evident in Bob's and Alice's research efforts. Bob failed to apply any standards of judgment. He did not review his book selection although book review indexes were on his instructor's list; he simply did not understand their importance. His choice of periodical articles reveals that he was unable to recognize the proper level of research materials to be used for his paper and differentiate between popular and scholarly sources. Alice carefully selected the types of information she needed and compiled a bibliography that consisted of scholarly, popular, and current materials. Depending on the depth of Alice's paper, she might elect to locate one or more key sources and use them to locate additional pertinent information.

Bob's and Alice's respective information gathering skills illustrate the substantive difference between a skill-based and a concept-based approach to research. The application of concepts — question analysis, information growth and use, and evaluation — is pivotal to research. Alice has the conceptual tools in addition to the physical ones to create a unique search strategy for her topic. Bob is struggling to fit his topic into a fixed pattern of research.

Using concepts as the basis for identifying information needs (question analysis), anticipating sources and research patterns (discipline growth and scholarly communication), and refining the selection of materials (evaluation and judgment) are requisites for thorough and complete research. Additionally, they build the foundations for transference of research skills.

The ability to transfer learning is one of the most desirable outcomes of the teaching process. In research strategies, transference of research skills can be achieved partially by providing models that are not tool or subject specific but organic in nature. As research needs change, these concepts can be reshaped. These concepts ensure that students understand not only the "where" of information, but more importantly the "how" of information development and the "why" of selection and evaluation of information. These conceptual tools give students the ability to separate knowledge from information. This crucial distinction — that "knowledge is orderly and cumulative, information is random and miscellaneous" (Boorstin, 1982, p. 54) — may well be the distinguishing factor in both preparation and evaluation of printed sources.

Developing students' abilities to formulate search strategies has been and continues to be a goal of library instruction. The present shift in emphasis, from the fixed, static search strategy to the dynamic search strategy, reinforces the reality of research, which is flexible, malleable, and distinct. Learning about information development, information use, information quality, and the relationship between information and information control along with traditional information tools validates these patterns of research as conceptual frameworks for instruction. Although these research concepts are not new, their application to instruction is; they should be central to library instruction. Then, and only then, can search strategy fulfill its potential.

References

Beaubien, A. K., Hogan, S. A., George, M. W. *Learning the Library: Concepts and Methods for Effective Bibliographic Instruction.* New York: Bowker, 1982.

Boorstin, D. J. "Homo Up-to-Datum Is a Dunce." *Reader's Digest,* 1982, *120* (9), 54–56.

Frick, E. "Information Structure and Bibliographic Instruction." *Journal of Academic Librarianship,* 1975, *1* (4), 12–14.

Frick, E. "Teaching Information Structure: Turning Dependent Researchers into Self-Teachers." In C. Oberman and K. Strauch (Eds.), *Theories of Bibliographic Education: Designs for Teaching.* New York: Bowker, 1982.

Garfield, E. "Is Information Retrieval in the Arts and Humanities Inherently Different from That in Science? The Effect That ISI's Citation Index for the Arts and Humanities Is Expected to Have on Future Scholarship." *Library Quarterly,* 1980, *50* (1), 40–57.

Hopkins, F. L. "Bibliographic Instruction: An Emerging Professional Discipline." In C. A. Kirkendall (Ed.), *Directions for the Decade: Library Instruction in the 1980s.* Ann Arbor, Mich.: Pierian Press, 1981.

Keresztesi, M. "The Science of Bibliography: Theoretical Implications for Bibliographic Instruction." In C. Oberman and K. Strauch (Eds.), *Theories of Bibliographic Education: Designs for Teaching.* New York: Bowker, 1982.

Kobelski, P., and Reichel, M. "Conceptual Frameworks for Bibliographic Instruction." *Journal of Academic Librarianship,* 1981, *7* (2), 73–77.

MacGregor, J., and McInnis, R. G. "Integrating Classroom Instruction and Library Research: The Cognitive Functions of Bibliographic Network Structures." *Journal of Higher Education,* 1977, *48* (1), 17–38.

McInnis, R. G. *New Perspectives for Reference Service in Academic Libraries.* Westport, Conn.: Greenwood Press, 1978.

Oberman, C. "Question Analysis and the Learning Cycle." *Research Strategies,* 1983, *1* (1).

Rogers, S. J. "Research Strategies: Bibliographic Instruction for Undergraduates." *Library Trends,* 1980, *29* (1), 69–82.

Smalley, T. N. "Bibliographic Instruction in Academic Libraries: Questioning Some Assumptions." *Journal of Academic Librarianship,* 1977, *3* (5), 280–283.

Smalley, T. N., and Plum, S. H. "Teaching Library Researching in the Humanities and the Sciences: A Contextual Approach." In C. Oberman and K. Strauch (Eds.), *Theories of Bibliographic Education: Designs for Teaching.* New York: Bowker, 1982.

Smith, L. C. "Citation Analysis." *Library Trends,* 1981, *30* (1), 83–106.

Cerise Oberman is head of reference and assistant professor at the Walter Library, University of Minnesota, Twin Cities. She is co-editor of Theories for Bibliographic Education: Designs for Teaching *(Bowker, 1982).*

The term paper is the faculty's traditional method of engaging students in library use. However there are a variety of alternatives which can accomplish the same objective.

Alternatives to the Term Paper

Evan I. Farber

Where or when the use of the term paper began would make an interesting study, perhaps even a good topic for a term paper in a history of education course. While the history of the term paper is not the topic of this chapter, it is safe to say that the term paper has been around a long time and that contention about its usefulness and arguments for and against its effectiveness as a teaching device have been around almost as long. In an article by Suzzallo in *A Cyclopedia of Education,* published between 1911 and 1914, he points out that the library method ". . . represents an extreme reaction from the slavish use of a class text, distinctly in the right direction. The teacher who relies largely upon one or more texts is very likely not to give the student power to investigate and develop a subject under the difficulties which would confront him, once he is removed from teachers and school facilities. . . . The library method bears somewhat the same relation to the modern humanities as the laboratory method does to the modern natural sciences; it makes the pupil familiar with the materials and methods which would be used in the more thoroughgoing field of research" (vol. 4, p. 23). It is that last mentioned aspect of the term paper—familiarizing students with the materials and methods of research—that is the topic of this chapter.

The Term Paper as a Teaching Device

The term paper as a teaching device has been written about extensively (see Ford and others, 1982, which identifies over 200 articles, mostly in fresh-

T. G. Kirk (Ed.). *Increasing the Teaching Role of Academic Libraries.*
New Directions for Teaching and Learning, no. 18. San Francisco: Jossey-Bass, June 1984.

man composition courses). Here, we are primarily concerned with assignments in courses beyond the level of most freshmen and so assume that the students who are given these assignments have already acquired some basic information about using the library.

Perhaps we should first ask why instructors use term papers so readily — what value do they see in them? If so many instructors use them as a standard assignment, why should they consider alternatives?

In discussing the purposes and shortcomings of term papers, one cannot do any better than consult an article written over forty years ago by Harry N. Rivlin (1942) that summarizes responses of faculty at Queens College, New York. The report was concerned "only with the preparation of a major term paper," for which faculty saw as objectives to be achieved: "to give able students an opportunity to do systematic, critical, or constructive work independently, under the guidance of the instructor; to supplement the student's knowledge of the field by wider reading and thinking," and "to enable the student to explore more fully some phase of the course in which he or she has a special interest... yet which should not take up too much time of the class" (p. 314–315). It is interesting to note that while none of the faculty responses suggested improved library skills as an objective, a group of seniors who were asked to discuss term papers from the student's viewpoint "referred most often to the value of training in research procedures. Many of them mentioned the improvement in their ability to use the library effectively" (p. 316).

The faculty members had a number of suggestions for improving the quality of term papers: schedule bibliographies and progress reports, restrict term paper assignments to advanced elective courses, use them only as an integral part of the course, and offer students a wide variety of topics. All of these are, of course, useful suggestions, but later in the article Rivlin makes this salient point:

> More extensive use may be made of various substitutes for the term paper. In many instances the actual writing of the paper is the least valuable part of the entire undertaking.... What the substitute assignment should be will depend almost entirely on the nature of the course, the composition of the class, and the special needs to be met by the assignment. If the assignment aims at introducing the student to bibliographic research, he may gain as much from the preparation of an annotated bibliography.... All of us will admit that the term paper is sometimes used as a convenient and academically respected means of meeting a need that can be satisfied as well, and possibly better, by other types of assignments (pp. 319–320).

His conclusion is that "the term paper is a worthwhile college assignment provided it is no *pro forma* assignment, but rather one that is carefully adjusted to attain specific aims and one that is reasonably supervised during its preparation." Every reference librarian could applaud this; the term paper can be a rewarding experience and of real educational significance, but, for the purposes of teaching students to make effective use of library materials or to improve their research skills, one has to acknowledge the common sense in Rivlin's recognition that other types of assignments may be better than the term paper.

Alternatives to the Term Paper

The crucial question, then, is: What kinds of assignments can be devised that have some of the acknowledged educational benefits of the term paper, avoid its disadvantages, and, at the same time, do a better job of extending students' knowledge of and skills in using library resources? The answer is, of course, that there's no limit to the variety of such assignments; they will, as Rivlin noted, "depend almost entirely on the nature of the course, the composition of the class, and the special needs to be met by the assignment." Surely one must add that they also depend on the flexibility of instructors' attitudes toward new kinds of assignments and, even more important, willingness to work with an instructional librarian in devising and implementing such assignments.

To illustrate this variety, a number of assignments that have been used in courses at Earlham College are discussed. (For background on Earlham College's program see Rader, this volume). All were devised by a librarian and the teaching faculty member working together.

The Annotated Bibliography. The annotated bibliography is hardly a novel assignment, and it is surely one of the most frequently used alternatives; the possible variations in its implementation are manifold. Here are three examples.

Example One. In a Shakespeare course at Earlham College, the class read nine of Shakespeare's plays during the term. For their final written assignment, the students first had to identify a critical problem in one of the plays and, using the bibliographical apparatus, come up with twenty articles, books, or essays that discussed that problem. From those twenty, students were to select six of the best sources that covered the full range of the problem and annotate these six.

The discussion between the librarian and the instructor began with the idea of doing an annotated bibliography, since all students had done at least one such bibliography in prior courses. The instructor felt that the students ought to be able to find twenty good sources, but the librarian felt that having to annotate all of them would take too much time. Since both instructor and librarian wanted the students to have to choose only the best sources and read those carefully, six sources seemed a reasonable number. The reason for asking for at least two recently published ones was so students would not depend only on standard undergraduate guides to Shakespeare but would have to look through indexes and annual bibliographies published since those guides.

Since the course consisted of upperclass students, all of whom presumably knew how to use the library well, the lecture was brief. The students were made aware of the vast number of publications on Shakespeare and the importance of using guides to the literature. The handouts consisted of an annotated listing of reference materials on Shakespeare, a two-page guide on how to write annotations, a few samples of good annotations taken from *Choice* magazine, and a standard annotated bibliography on Shakespeare's tragedies.

Example Two. In a political science course, American foreign policy, students were instructed as follows:

> Your assignment is to work in groups of three and to assemble and critically evaluate material from public and governmental information sources on a particular foreign policy issue. At three different times during the term you will turn in a different part of the project, with the entire opus due on May 23. Accompanying your annotated bibliography at that time will be a fifteen-page interpretive essay that examines the ideological conflicts over the issue, a brief history of the issue, the actors involved in the policy formulation process, the other foreign policy issues to which your topic is linkied, and a brief statement about the future of your foreign policy issue.

The reasons for assigning group projects were four: (1) it was a very large class, so the number of topics could be fewer; (2) the instructor believed that students should learn to work cooperatively; (3) the assignment was a large one, and division of labor might help reduce the amount of time spent on it; and (4) discussions within a group could provide a learning experience in itself.

The librarian's instruction to the class included the presentation of a search strategy and the use of government documents; handouts included an annotated listing of relevant reference materials and a two-page guide on how to write annotations.

Example Three. Another variation of the annotated bibliography assignment was made in an introduction to philosophy course which focused on sexual ethics. The students were asked to find several important articles on affirmative action and to make sure that the articles took different positions. They then annotated the two most important differing articles and related them to their own ethical theories. The librarian's presentation again was based on a sample search that used standard indexes the students should have been already familiar with; the *Philosopher's Index,* the *Encyclopedia of Philosophy,* and a few specialized bibliographies relevant for the topics were added.

The library aims in these assignments are obvious. Students learn a new range of reference materials and, thus, begin to understand that for every topic there is an appropriate body of reference works. Students also recognize that a major problem in searching for information on almost any topic is not one of finding enough information but of finding too much and being forced to select. They also learn that one of the most useful kinds of reference works is the one that helps sort out the important materials. Finally, students realize that even with these guides, one must apply certain criteria in making choices. Finally, the reason for using a sample search in most cases is to get students to understand that there is a systematic way of finding information.

From the instructor's viewpoint, the assignments meant that students investigated a specific topic in some depth, learned that there were varied or even conflicting interpretations, and, ultimately, because they neeed to decide which were most important, developed their own criteria on the subject.

The "Practical" Assignment. A very different kind of assignment is one that has a practical aspect. Obviously, such assignments are not appropriate in all courses, but for those where they are, there is a special appeal for students. Below are a few examples:

Example One. In a course in children's literature, each student was asked to describe a class they would like to teach—the grade, the socioeconomic level, and so on. Then they were asked to select $100 worth of children's books appropriate for that class. The library instruction introduced them to the bibliographies, indexes, and selection tools for children's literature, and the students had to justify each choice. The practical aspects are two: (1) the assignment posits a situation that a teacher might encounter; and (2) it introduces the students, all prospective teachers, to tools they can use in their careers.

Example Two. One of the most unusual practical assignments was given in a course on animal behavior for advanced biology and psychology majors. All of these students know how to use the material in their respective disciplines, but in this case they were asked to design an experiment in the field of animal behavior nutrition that would attempt to ask and answer a question so meaningful that a government agency or a research institute might want to fund it. They were asked to identify an appropriate funding agency, figure out the costs involved, and then submit a proposal describing their project along with a supporting annotated bibliography. Groups of students acted as reviewers for the proposals.

Since the students already know the reference literature in their disciplines, the library instruction was limited to showing them material on foundations and other sources of funding and material on the writing of proposals.

Example Three. An innovative and highly successful assignment was one called "Reasonable Patienthood." It has been given in a human biology course taken by students who were not biology majors but who had had an introductory course in biology. The class usually has about eighty students. The students were given a listing of about seventy-five diagnosed conditions and prescribed treatments, with examples ranging from the most common and trivial jock itch—tolnaftate, sore throat—Listerine) to the most serious (Parkinson's Disease—L-dopa, breast cancer—radical mastectomy). They were then instructed to, "as a responsible patient, investigate the nature of your diagnosed condition and the effectiveness of the prescribed treatment." In the end product, a two-page paper, the following items were to be covered: a description of the condition and its symptoms, the disease's etiology, its prognosis, evidence of the effectiveness of the prescribed treatment and its side effects and contraindications; and a comparison of the relative effectiveness of alternate treatments. In addition, each student was to give a ten-minute oral report on this paper.

The lab manual for the course included a chapter on this assignment. In that chapter was the list of diagnosed conditions and an annotated bibliography of sources for finding biological and medical information. Since the students had been instructed in an earlier course about using the biological literature, the librarian in this course simply reminded them about the materials and focused on the literature of medicine.

Not many assignments can have such personal, immediate interest to students as this one. Its results, though, are instructive. Even though the course is a demanding one and this assignment an intensive one, most students completed it readily and enthusiastically, and the comments on this assignment in the course evaluations were overwhelmingly positive.

In this case, the library objectives are minimal—simply getting students to be aware of another, very different body of reference materials.

Example Four. Students were asked in an advanced psychology course to select a specific topic that interested them (REM sleep) and that had been treated in a review article within the past five years or so. They were then asked to update the review of the literature in light of articles published since the earlier review was written.

The library instruction involved a sample search on an appropriate topic, beginning with the review article and then illustrating how to update it by using citation indexes and *Psychological Abstracts.* The lecture material during the session centered on the function of a review article, the rationale and mechanics of citation indexes, and the differences, in terms of their theory and structure, between citation indexes and traditional indexes and abstracting services. The practicality of the assignment was that it made students go through the same process a professional must go through before doing any experimental research.

Evaluating Scholarship. Surely an important part of teaching undergraduates is getting students to understand the process of scholarship. The foregoing assignments made students replicate part of that process. Other assignments described below focus on the way scholars examine and evaluate the materials of scholarship.

Example One. In an introductory course on United States history, the instructor asked students to examine primary materials on slave life or events of the abolition movement and compare them with the textbook's treatment of those subjects. The students were then to write their own brief accounts of those aspects or events. The librarian compiled a bibliography of guides to sources on slave life and the pre-Civil War period — biographical dictionaries and indexes, bibliographies of biographies and autobiographies, newspaper indexes, *Poole's Index,* and the *Index to the American Slave* — and the lecture consisted primarily of comments on these sources. This was a relatively simple assignment but a productive and interesting one for students. It made them look at primary sources, and then see how a text used or misused such sources. From the librarian's perspective, it helped show students, once again, that there are ways of finding materials — both through bibliographies or indexes and guides to the literature — that are more effective than just the card catalogue.

Example Two. In a more advanced history course, one on East Asian history, students were given a list of books, all of which were significant contributions to the interpretation of major events or movements in East Asia. After having read any one of the books, each student was asked to get as much information about the author as possible, gather reactions to the book through book reviews, and then find information about the reviewers. The end product was to be a relatively short paper on the book's interpretation of the event, which would take into account all the information gathered. The handouts given to the students by the librarian included descriptions of the various book review indexes and biographical sources and a strategy for searching them.

Again, this was a relatively simple assignment but useful from both the instructor's and the librarian's viewpoints. Students were made to realize, perhaps for the first time, that scholars can disagree honestly and openly, and thus could understand the crucial role of reviews in the scholarly process. They also learned the importance of knowing the author's and the reviewer's credentials and perspectives and how to find information about these. A similar assignment has been used for other courses in history and political science.

Example Three. This final example from an American government course represents perhaps the ideal library-based assignment. It achieves both the objectives of the instructor and of the librarian, both sets of objectives being so integral to the assignment and to the course that they have a truly symbiotic relationship. The following is from the course syllabus:

> This project is designed to develop an understanding of the process of government in the United States through direct researching in the primary documents of that government. You will examine in detail the development of an idea or a proposal from its inception in Congress or the Executive [Branch] through its legislative career in both Houses of Congress.... This study will be accompanied, of course, by the normal classroom lectures and discussion and by the reading of secondary texts.
>
> The final term paper will be a narrative that analyzes the partic-

ular aspects of the process that had significance in the outcome of the bill. It is hoped that this study will provide you with a more intimate and "firsthand" knowledge and "feel" for the governmental process than would be gleaned by the secondary sources only.

Knowledge of the skills of information retrieval in these valuable sources can be a major research tool to students of political science. A second purpose of this term project, therefore, is to develop these skills in the discovery and use of government documents and relevant reference material in the library.

Students were divided into groups of four or five (in order to reduce the number of legislative items and to encourage them to share ideas), and, using a worksheet that provided spaces for all the necessary factual information, they then prepared a narrative account of the legislative history of the bill. They needed to find (and the library instruction showed them how) and use information in *CQ Weekly Report* and the Serial Set, and to use such indexes as the *Monthly Catalog* and *CIS,* that provide access to those sources.

From the instructor's viewpoint, the students gained insight into the political process by using these primary sources. Furthermore, the knowledge gained of government documents was useful in later courses. From the librarian's viewpoint, the government documents collection, consigned in many libraries to an obscure corner of the stacks or used primarily by graduate students and faculty, became an important part of the undergraduate collection, and its usefulness for other courses and other disciplines was easy to implement.

This was an assignment, then, planned to further both the instructor's and the librarian's sets of objectives, and those objectives were mutually reinforcing in the assignment's implementation. By learning about the process of government, students also learned about their source materials. By learning about the source materials, students saw the process of government at work. Such an assignment, however, could be devised only by the librarian and the instructor working together, each aware of and sympathetic to the objectives of the other.

Conclusion

It is important to reiterate that the term paper can be an appropriate and useful assignment, not only from the instructor's vantage point but from the librarian's. If it is to be appropriate and useful, however, the assignment must include five elements: (1) a staging of the process, so that students cannot use only a few sources just prior to writing the paper; (2) students must have sufficient expertise in the subject to permit them to evaluate materials they find in order for them to make valid inferences; (3) the requirements for the paper's length must be realistic; (4) the subjects chosen by the students need to be guided so that they are not too broad as to be unmanageable yet not so narrow as to be trivial or to lack material; and (5) the institution's library resources must be considered, not only their availability but also their accessibility by students at their particular level. If these elements can be addressed satisfactorily, then, the term paper can be worthwhile.

At the same time instructors should recognize that assignments other than the term paper may be more productive and educationally valid, particularly in improving the library skills of their students. Certainly assignments can be made more interesting to students for whom term papers have become something to be endured. What is needed are instructors with initiative, imagination, and the willingness to recognize that librarians have a real concern for their students' education and can help in devising and implementing new approaches to the teaching and learning process.

References

Ford, J., Rees, S., and Wood, D. "Research Paper Instruction: Comprehensive Bibliography of Periodical Sources, 1923–1980." *Bulletin of Bibliography,* 1982, *34,* 84–98.
Rivlin, H. N. "The Writing of Term Papers." *Journal of Higher Education,* 1942, *13,* 314–320.
Suzzallo, H. "Library Method." In P. Monroe (Ed.), *A Cyclopedia of Education.* New York: Macmillan, 1911–1914.

Evan I. Farber has been head librarian at Earlham College, Richmond, Indiana since 1962. Academic Librarian of the Year in 1980, he has been president of the Association of College and Research Libraries. In addition to numerous articles and presentations on bibliographic instruction, he is author of Classified List of Periodicals for the College Library, *and editor of a festschrift for Guy R. Lyle.*

Librarians can promote and improve their programs of
bibliographic instruction through a faculty development
effort on appropriate undergraduate use of the college library.

The Faculty/Librarian Partnership

Rose Ann Simon

More than one faculty member who has assigned a library research paper, offered suggestions for readings, and advised students to consult the librarian for help in finding other material has received, for his pains, a number of disappointing research papers. Even the upperclass student (whom experience has taught to construct coherent summaries of material) often fails to use a judicious selection of sources on the topic. But in the same way that few undergraduates have learned to transcend mere summary and formulate new questions, few have learned a research methodology that leads them to a profitable variety of resources. How, then, is a faculty member, committed to the development of student skills in independent bibliographic research, to foster that development?

The faculty member cannot simply pass along the lessons in library research learned as an undergraduate, because most of the research training was at the graduate level. Even there, the instruction in identifying and locating key resources was largely informal, haphazard, and not comprehensive. The emphasis was not on general or interdisciplinary background, but on increasingly specialized studies leading to original, rather than summary, research. By the time the faculty member finished the dissertation he or she had devoted several years to a research project that represented distinctly new thought and work. Thus, the type of research learned and carried out in a major university library is highly unlike the type of research of undergraduate students in their own library. It is not clear what the faculty member should

T. G. Kirk (Ed.). *Increasing the Teaching Role of Academic Libraries.*
New Directions for Teaching and Learning, no. 18. San Francisco: Jossey-Bass, June 1984.

tell students about using the college library, particularly since the typical faculty member in any college has had little opportunity to see or use the college library as a library designed specifically for the research use of undergraduate students. The efforts to provide solid guidance in the use of that resource are therefore restricted by this fundamental lack of familiarity with the college library.

The person who knows the library intimately is the librarian. The librarian knows the collections, the systems, and the strengths and weaknesses of both. But the librarian does not know what the objectives of the class assignment are, what the faculty member expects the student to do, and what the faculty member has actually told the student. Nothing the student says about any of these things is necessarily complete or even accurate. The student's own lack of experience in completing a valid research project is the biggest obstacle to successful mastery of the process, including the identification and location of prime library resources. As talented and dedicated as the librarian may be, the ability to help the student complete the assignment depends first upon the student's willingness to ask for help (many are not) and then upon the student's comprehension of the assignment itself. Clearly, there is much to be gained in establishing a working partnership between faculty and librarians.

Objectives of Faculty/Librarian Partnership

The immediate objective of such a partnership is to share knowledge and insights into the local undergraduate research situation: What should the student be doing and learning? What library resources could be most helpful? How do students use the library and how should they use it? What do they need to be told in order to complete a research project successfully? The ultimate objective of the partnership is to create library research assignments that enhance not only the mastery of new subject matter but also the mastery of appropriate library resources. Whereas the typical research assignment is open ended (that is, most sources and research methods are unsepcified), the jointly planned assignment specifies certain resources and includes clear directions on how to use any library system. The selection of resources and systems depends on the faculty member's ultimate learning objectives for the course, but this is a knowledgeable choice based on a working familiarity with the college library as an undergraduate research facility. By enlisting the librarian as his consultant, the faculty member can gain perspective on the library research needed to help students master the research process.

For example, the whole question of how and where to begin the research inquiry reveals some important differences between faculty and librarian perceptions of student research. Some faculty members try to help their students get the research started by distributing a list of books on course topics. In individual cases, additional titles are recommended for student use. But the tacit assumptions are that either the lecture or the text provides sufficient background information on the topic, and that students can easily find an assortment of good books to fill out the picture. Belief in the first assumption is so strong that some faculty members delay making the assignment until nearly half of the course is over. Belief in the second fosters the tendency of students to use only circulating books as sources. Librarians can present some alternative methods for carrying out research projects.

Background material, for example, is readily available in a number of reference sources. General encyclopedias provide summaries, and subject encylopedias frequently present even more detailed discussions of course topics. These are excellent starting points for undergraduates, often surpassing lecture or textbook material on the same topic. Academics often show an aversion to encyclopedias, fearing that their summaries can be attractive to plagiarists. The fact that encyclopedia articles and undergraduate research papers might appear to be indistinguishable (especially to students) raises the question as to whether or not they are supposed to be so similar. If so, why not simply ask students to thoroughly learn the content of the appropriate encyclopedia articles? If not, then the process of gathering information for summary attains a degree of importance worthy of specific explanation. Students need to be told what kind of information to seek and how to shape a valid inquiry. They must comprehend the difference between their own papers and the summaries printed in encyclopedias.

Faculty members who can work with the librarians closely enough to examine this and related questions can come to better appreciate how to keep students from floundering in their library research projects. The faculty member can include instructions and advice that students need but have seldom received in most course assignments.

Even more important than the question of background resources is the one of student-selected sources for the project. Faculty members generally share their students' misplaced faith in the subject approach to the library's catalogue as the magic key to library research. This catalogue does identify the circulating materials on the consulted subject that are supposed to be in that library collection, and the system is good enough to foster the belief that it will lead the user to an acceptable amount of information. Undergraduates especially tend to eschew the option of seeking any additional information through any other, more complicated system. They have developed little appreciation for the importance of information found in any other way, particularly when faculty members have not expressed that importance. Consequently, major collections of resources — most notably periodicals and reference books — are under-utilized in most undergraduate research projects.

Librarians know only too well the limitations of access to library resources through the subject approach to the library's catalogue. Most would rejoice to help a faculty member see how students need to know the catalogue's limitations well enough to work around them. It does not take long to explain how to identify additional (sometimes more profitable) subject headings for consultation. Few faculty members have divined the significance of the entries at the bottom of catalogue cards or discovered the *Library of Congress Subject Headings* as a guide to the subject headings used in the library's catalogue. These are mysteries most long-time library users are delighted to solve, apply, and pass on to their students.

Without specific instructions, students tend to make distinctly limited use of library materials. Neither they nor their instructors know how to carry out a research methodology that is both comprehensive and appropriate for undergraduate study. Moreover, faculty members have had little opportunity to see how much and what type of guidance students need in order to carry out a responsible research project.

The faculty member who works with the librarian has the opportunity to explore, firsthand, materials and systems that students should be using profitably. The faculty member's direct experience with these matters allows them to identify the strengths and weaknesses of these systems for student projects. Papers can be very different when the student does not simply consult the library catalogue and rely on circulating monographs but also consults encyclopedias and handbooks, uses printed bibliographies, locates and uses review articles, uses indexes to periodicals, checks the library catalogue, and supplements the library's collection by using the interlibrary loan.

The librarian's methods may sound like extra effort, and it is important that a faculty member believe that the effort is worthwhile. Undergraduate education is distinguished by its attempt to make all readings immediately accessible to each student. Reserve shelves bulge because conscientious faculty members strive to leave nothing to chance; the student must have ready access to even the most peripheral suggested reading. Library research, however, leaves a great deal to chance. Every faculty member knows how much smaller the college library collection is than the graduate collection. There is a genuine desire to minimize the students' frustration (and consequent dissatisfaction) with the course requirements. As a result, faculty members have traditionally exercised a variety of research project options: (1) not to assign one at all, (2) to recommend reliance on a nearby research library, and (3) to grant tacit sanction to the students' reliance on a limited number of sources. Because of the value of knowing how to do independent bibliographic research, none of these options is a good one. What is necessary is to provide students with the necessary guidance in using what is, in most cases, a more than adequate undergraduate collection.

Library Research Projects as Faculty Development

It is important to explain that, while faculty members and librarians have been communicating along these lines for years, only a few institutions have made specific provision for improving the faculty member's working familiarity with the college library. Most programs of library research instruction enable the librarian to reach the students directly in some formal setting. But, insofar as research assignments are designed by the faculty member, the instructor's thorough knowledge of the library becomes a significant factor in the quality of instruction provided to the student.

To the extent that course assignments in library or bibliographic research contribute to the curricular goal of developing skills needed for life-long independent learning, undergraduate institutions bear responsibility for fostering the development of more effective library research assignments. The type of program that enables the faculty member to work with the librarian to learn how that library best serves student researchers represents a form of faculty development that deserves both earnest and significant support from the parent institution. Traditional funding priorities for faculty development include attendance at conferences and workshops, enrollment in refresher courses, and engagement in disciplinary research. Most of these projects involve travel, lodging, and equipment expenditures which represent the institution's investment in improved teaching. With budgets for such activities steadily shrinking, the advantages of the library research project are obvious: no travel is involved, and the necessary resources, including the consultant, are already available. The basic cost is payment to the faculty member for time—the amount of time needed to learn the library well and to produce a series of new research assignments that achieve course objectives more effectively than the old ones. A thorough program would require approximately 120 hours or some three to four weeks of steady effort. This time should be scheduled during the summer or, where applicable, during the January term since the faculty member should not be engaged in teaching or some other major project while working with the librarian. Similarly, provision should be made for the librarian to devote up to half the time to the program, depending on the number of faculty members in the program.

The first component of this program features the librarian as a short-term instructor who both teaches an ideal research strategy in the chosen discipline, and guides the faculty member through the actual process. It is necessary to demonstrate clearly and authentically what types of resources can be found in the college library besides those identified through the library's catalogue. Using this effective search strategy, the faculty member reviews the library's holdings in his discipline in all formats. Using established bibliographies and listings, the faculty member can gauge the strengths and weaknesses of the local collections and adjust assignments and expectations accordingly. The librarian can help the faculty member learn to use specific resources that he may be unfamiliar with but that are of great value in the preparation of coursework. It is true that many faculty members are reasonably familiar with those sections of the circulating collection that relate to their disciplines. But they are far less familiar with the corresponding reference materials that offer tremendous potential for creative and worthwhile research assignments. Librarians usually see the reference materials as the cream of the entire library collection, but few users are familiar with most of these apparently complicated, noncirculating items. Librarians are not only eager to share the secrets of this collection but also to offer suggestions for the application of these resources to coursework.

Ultimately, the faculty member brings all this new-found knowledge to bear on the formulation of course assignments that both ensure that students make use of particular resources or specific groups of resources and that they make use of them knowledgeably. The greatest drawback in the typical open-ended type of research assignment is the fact that it leaves so very much to chance — including the provision for the student learning to conduct a valid inquiry into a subject.

The results of this type of faculty development program have included some highly imaginative new assignments and some new, library-centered, courses. For example, students in a beginning-level physics course were asked to consult the appropriate biographical dictionaries for information on prominent physicists and to determine current figures for United States energy consumption and production from almanacs. Students in the same class received a two-page guide explaining how to find information for the course in periodicals. The guide included a briefly annotated list of selected index and periodical titles and an illustrated explanation of how to read the index citations and the serials catalogue entries. Students in another course on evolution were asked to work out part of Darwin's family tree using selected biographical resources. The instructor found that old issues of *Harper's Magazine* offered fascinating contemporary commentary and that atlases provided invaluable insight into the students' reading of *The Voyage of the Beagle*. Several faculty members presented clear, written explanations of the citation format preferred in their discipline with a statement explaining the obligation to document sources and the nature of plagiarism. This was designed to help students master the documentation phase of their research.

Thus, students were introduced to resources that enriched their course learning but that they would not have consulted without specific direction from the faculty member. Few faculty members, in the meantime, have enjoyed the luxury of planning a course with such an exciting variety of resources at their disposal. Few have had the opportunity to spend the time needed with the librarian and the resources. The time granted them to explore the library thoroughly and to learn its contents and systems under the experienced guidance of the professional librarian proved to be an invaluable investment in the faculty member's effectiveness as a creative teacher. Perhaps the final proof of this program's value has been its residual effects. These faculty members return to the library as they prepare for a new term of courses in order to spot resources useful in new assignments. They maintain frequent contact with the librarian, who is quick to apprise them of new acquisitions and to help work out some new student exercise. Considering the benefits to all concerned—faculty members, librarians, and students—this particular form of college faculty development probably represents one of the best academic bargains of the decade.

Rose Ann Simon is director of libraries at Salem Academy and College, Winston-Salem, North Carolina. Formerly she was on the staff of the Guilford College Library where she was project librarian for a Council on Library Resources Library Services Enhancement Grant.

There are a number of institutions, from small private colleges to large public universities, that have developed extensive bibliographic instruction programs.

Bibliographic Instruction Programs in Academic Libraries

Hannelore B. Rader

What makes an academic bibliographic instruction program successful? How does one establish and improve a bibliographic instruction program? Are there guidelines available to help academic librarians evaluate a particular bibliographic instruction program and its impact on library users?

Literally hundreds of academic bibliographic instruction programs have been developed in all types of colleges and universities during the last ten years because librarians, administrators, and faculty are becoming increasingly convinced that it is important to utilize existing library resources more effectively. Such utilization can only occur if library users are instructed in the most effective and efficient use of information resources, the structure of information within various disciplines, and the best information strategies.

Program Evaluation Criteria

What makes one bibliographic instruction program more successful than another? The answer to this question is difficult and complicated. Since no generally accepted evaluation guidelines exist at this time, the evaluation of the bibliographic instruction programs described here was based on the author's personal criteria derived from years of professional experience and input from many bibliographic instruction experts in the United States,

T. G. Kirk (Ed.). *Increasing the Teaching Role of Academic Libraries.*
New Directions for Teaching and Learning, no. 18. San Francisco: Jossey-Bass, June 1984.

Canada and Europe as well as the LOEX national clearinghouse, and available program information (Rader, 1976). (Detailed information on the programs described is available from LOEX Clearinghouse, Center for Education Resources, Eastern Michigan University, Ypsilanti, Michigan 48197.) The programs included here vary widely in format, purpose, and accomplishments but share, above all, several factors for success: enthusiasm, commitment to students, longevity, and faculty and administrative support. The criteria used to select the described bibliographic instruction programs can be summarized as follows:

1. *Duration of Program.* The program has been in existence for five or more years.
2. *Administrative Support.* The administration understands the concept of library instruction, its value for students, the faculty's role in it, its relationship to the institution's objectives, and, furthermore, the administration is concerned enough about the importance of library instruction to provide personnel, funds, and other institutional support for a library instruction program.
3. *Faculty Support and Cooperation.* Faculty support for library instruction usually involves course-related activities. The librarian and instructor cooperate in a given course that includes library research, and the librarian teaches students the needed library skills to do the research. This type of cooperation requires that the instructor realizes the need for library skills and recognizes the librarian's expertise in teaching students such skills. Furthermore, the instructor must realize the importance of library instruction to the extent of devoting actual class time to it.
4. *Integration into the Campus Curriculum.* Bibliographic instruction modules are incorporated into faculty's course syllabi on a regular basis and become part of the course objectives and grade.
5. *Program Goals and Objectives.* The bibliographic instruction program is based on a set of goals and objectives developed on each campus according to needs and available resources.
6. *Comprehensiveness of Program.*
   A. Progression from orientation to services and facilities, through basic library skills instruction to advanced bibliographic instruction in all subject areas
   B. Use of a variety of instructional methodology (course-related, credit courses, programmed instruction, workshops, point-of-use modules)
   C. Use of a variety of instructional materials (television, workbooks, exercises, guides, software, slides, tapes)
7. *Impact of Program.*
   A. Statistical evidence
      1. Library use (reference, circulation, interlibrary loan, collection development)

2. Number of students reached (classes, disciplines, faculty)
3. Number of instructional materials produced and used
B. Evaluation of program
   1. Evaluation of librarians as teachers
   2. Program impact on student and faculty attitudes toward the library
   3. Changes within the program
   4. Faculty evaluation of program (has program influenced faculty's way of teaching or the curriculum?)
C. *Growth of Program.* The bibliographic instruction program begins small and continues to expand with generated demand. It also continues to change with user needs as assessed on a regular basis
D. Likelihood of program's continuation

Using these criteria, the eleven bibliographic instruction programs are explored below.

Berea College

Berea College located in Berea, Kentucky, is a small, private liberal arts college with an enrollment of 1,500 students. As an integral part of the educational program, students are expected to work on the campus to maintain it. The director of Hutchins Library is Thomas Kirk; Phyllis Hughes, the head of reference, directs the user instruction program.

History. The user instruction program has been in existence since 1974–1975 when plans called for a tape tour of the library and a freshman conference project. Also planned were special audio self-instruction units for subject literature and search strategies for upper-class level courses. Constraints in staffing due to low budget support limited the development of the upper-level audio instruction project. However, the library tape tour and the tutorial conferences for the freshman research instruction program based on individualized hands-on instruction have been successfully utilized at Berea College since 1975 (Hughes and Flandreau, 1980). In 1980–1981 the user instruction program was changed; the change was significantly guided by the philosophy that all library instruction should be "course-related, graduated, and frequent enough to have cumulative impact."

Current Program Description. The user instruction program is coordinated through a number of committees under the direction of Phyllis Hughes and involves all professional staff for from 25 percent to 50 percent of their time. The program features these components:

1. Since the college's general education programs require that students obtain library research skills as freshmen, instructional units for the freshman composition and the freshman seminar courses were developed by the library staff. In freshman composition, students are instructed by a tape that reviews the mechanics of using ency-

clopedias, the card catalogue and *Readers' Guide*, exercises, and class discussions. The freshman seminars include the use of a bibliography that features general reference sources specific to each seminar topic, a lecture on search strategy, use of card catalogue and indexes, a topic-specific exercise, and an individual conference-reference interview after completion of the exercise.

2. Other general education courses, particularly the cultural area requirement courses, include required library research. For these the library staff develop instruction bibliographies and provide in-class instruction built on the freshman program.

3. A third component of the program is targeted at selected courses in each department. The objective is to teach the specialized tools and literature reserach strategies of the students' major field. This program utilizes the library instruction tapes that were begun in 1975–1976, as well as printed bibliographies, lectures, and exercises.

The entire user instruction program is designed to meet students' immediate needs while teaching them principles of bibliographic organization and the relationship of literature types. In addition to the audio tapes, lectures and exercises are also used to teach students bibliographic skills. Statistics for the program indicate that it has grown each year and that 27 percent of the students are involved in the instruction program.

Bernard M. Baruch College of the City University of New York

Baruch College, located in New York City, is a state-supported business and liberal arts college and has an enrollment of 14,000 undergraduates and graduate students. Business, public administration, and education are emphasized. The library is an academic department headed by Alan Weiner (acting). The library instruction program is coordinated by the Deputy for Library Instruction, Thomas Atkins.

History. The library instruction program at Baruch College began in 1970 when it was decided to replace the usual library orientation lecture with an elective credit course that was taught for the first time in 1974. The course became very popular during the 1970s and evolved into a basic library skills course and an advanced course. By 1980, the three-credit basic skills course had become so popular that eleven sections of thirty-five students each were taught while the one-credit advance course had much lower enrollments. These courses were reaching about 20 percent of the freshman class. The course uses a textbook written by two staff members (Atkins and Langstaff, 1979). In addition, course-related library instruction was developed around specific assignments and in cooperation with faculty. In 1979–1980, Baruch College began to receive a Title III grant to develop an in-depth library research instruction program for undergraduates.

Current Program Description. The library instruction program at

Baruch College is designed around a number of library research credit courses (a three-credit basic skills course and a two-credit advanced online information retrieval course). The courses utilize exercises, tapes, a textbook, transparencies, bibliographies, and literature guides. Through these credit courses, 30 percent of freshmen receive basic library skills instruction.

The course-related library instruction program reaches an additional 4,000 students annually. A number of very successful workshops and seminars are also offered to both freshmen and upper-level students to give them bibliographic guidance. A variety of print and media materials have been developed into teaching packages (Rothstein and McDonough, 1982).

A library lab, duplicating a reference library for teaching purposes, has been set up to give students hands-on experience with many reference tools. Workshops that utilize trained student volunteers are offered in this lab.

Earlham College

Earlham College, located in Richmond, Indiana, is a small, private liberal arts college with an enrollment of 1,100 students. In addition to traditional programs, curriculum offerings include special programs in wilderness, museum studies, peace and conflict studies, and foreign studies. The director of the Lilly Library and the Wildman Science Library is Evan Farber. All professional staff members are involved in library instruction.

History. The conversion of Earlham College's library to a teaching library began as early as 1962 and was based on the realization that students were unable to find information and performed poorly on library-related assignments and that library resources were not utilized enough. Throughout the last twenty years, the library staff has worked closely with the faculty to participate more fully in the teaching and learning process on campus.

Current Program Description. Librarians prepare bibliographies, teach class sessions on how to find and use materials, and work with students on an individual basis to help them gain basic library skills. All students are assessed as to their basic library skills when they first come to Earlham. Those found lacking in basic library skills are tutored individually by reference librarians. The faculty has overwhelmingly endorsed the bibliographic instruction program by making competence in the skills of information retrieval and the use of the library for research purposes one of thirteen educational goals of the curriculum set by the faculty (Farber, 1974). The library instruction program has become totally integrated into the curriculum and is based on a progressive levels approach. The program is course-and-assignment related and retains a remarkable flexibility. Librarians and faculty work closely together to structure the library instruction to fit course objectives. Lectures, bibliographies, and exercises are utilized most of the time. The Earlham program has been described repeatedly (Kennedy, 1970; Kennedy and others, 1971) and continues to serve as a model and inspiration for academic librarians interested in setting up or improving a bibliographic instruction program.

Lake Forest College

Lake Forest College, located in Lake Forest, Illinois, is a small, private liberal arts college and has an enrollment of about 1,000 undergraduate and graduate students. Arthur H. Miller is the director of Donnelley Library and Joann H. Lee is the head of reader services and coordinates the library instruction program.

History. Though library user education at Lake Forest College has been around for many years, it became more structured and more closely tied to the faculty and the curriculum in 1977 when the library received two grants from the Council on Library Resources and the National Endowment for the Humanities. The grants provided the library staff with an opportunity to develop more specialized programs of bibliographic instruction in cooperation with the faculty. Library skills packages were developed for the freshman composition courses and tailored to each faculty member's needs; this in turn created a network of faculty-student-librarian interactions. Students are taught to use increasingly difficult library resources in individual courses but without the guidance of a librarian. Because of the grants, the librarians were also able to develop a bibliographic instruction component with an emphasis on on-line data base searching (Lee, 1980).

Current Program Description. The bibliographic instruction program at Lake Forest College is a multilevel course-integrated program based on student need and motivation and structured as follows:

1. At the introductory level, library instruction is presented in composition courses by using a number of guides similar to those used at the University of Texas at Austin. Students are guided through their first library research paper assignment by each composition instructor. The library staff participates in the preparation of materials and evaluation.

2. At the intermediate level, students take various library courses before beginning their major. Through participatory small group instruction, librarians instruct students in a limited number of pertinent sources and students are taught to use the basic search strategy. Politics, local and regional studies, economics, and sociology are the courses in which this type of instruction is usually given.

3. At the advanced level of the library instruction program, on-line data base searching is used as an instructional device. Workshops are given to students to familiarize them with on-line searching of periodical data bases. Students are taught how to structure their search strategies. Evaluation is accomplished by assessing students' research progress as reflected in their papers. Faculty and librarians work closely together to plan and implement the advanced level instruction (Lee and Miller, 1981).

Ohio State University

Ohio State University, located in Columbus, Ohio, is a large, comprehensive, state-supported university that has sixteen colleges, 117 departments, and an enrollment of 53,000 students. The library system is large and complex and includes twenty-nine libraries and 3.6 million volumes. A special feature of the library system is the Library Control System (LCS), a computerized catalogue system that links all the libraries with the State Library of Ohio. LCS provides information on all library holdings and circulation status. William Studer is the director of the Ohio State University libraries and Virginia Tiefel is the director of library user education.

History. In 1978, the position of director of library user education (DLUE) was created at Ohio State University because the library faculty felt strongly that students did not know how to use libraries and did not have the necessary information skills to do basic research at the university. The DLUE was responsible for the coordination and development of a comprehensive, sequential-level user education program and acted as a liaison between classroom and library faculty. A Council on User Education was created to serve a communication and advisory function for user education in Ohio State University's library system. Goals and objectives were established for several levels of the instruction program. Faculty seminars have been sponsored by the library faculty to inform classroom faculty about course-related library instruction and to begin the process of integrating library instruction with the curriculum.

Current Program Description. The Ohio State University bibliographic instruction program has several components and is structured to progress from a basic to an advanced level. On the basic level, a formal program of library instruction teaches freshman students basic library skills. Approximately 9,000 freshmen are reached with the Library Instruction Program (LIP) in which information packets, exercises, and lectures are utilized (Kerker and others, 1981). A quarterly newsletter *CLUE* (Comments on Library User Education), is produced to provide information on library instruction activities in this large library system. Since 1982, LIP also includes the use of a videotape, "Battle of the Library Superstars," that was produced at Ohio State University by library and telecommunication staff. This award-winning tape is both informative and entertaining and is used by librarians in classroom instruction; this tape received unanimous praise from students, faculty, administrators, and librarians. To allow students to learn to use the library system independently, a chapter on the library that includes information and exercises has been included in the *University Survey: A Guidebook for New Students 1982–83.* The freshman library instruction program is carried out by the undergraduate librarians with volunteer help from the library faculty on campus. LIP is continuously evaluated in order to refine the program and assess its impact on students and the library (Pearson and Tiefel, 1982).

Students' research abilities are further developed through course-integrated library instruction in sophomore- and junior-level courses, and a Graduate Student Handbook has been developed for future use to teach graduate students needed library skills. This program continues to grow annually, especially as a result of the faculty colloquia sponsored by the library staff each year. Three faculty colloquia have been held for classroom faculty; a fourth is planned for 1983 and will, for the first time, be open to participants from outside the university. The colloquia have addressed special topics of interest to classroom faculty that are related to student research and related library needs. These colloquia have given classroom faculty an opportunity to discuss problems among themselves and help them become more aware of the role the library can play in the teaching and learning process. As a result of these colloquia, additional departments at Ohio State University are moving into multi-level, curriculum-integrated library instruction each year.

State University of New York College at Brockport

State University College at Brockport in Brockport, New York, is a medium-sized state institution that offers a variety of degree programs with an emphasis on the social sciences. The enrollment is approximately 7,000 students. George W. Cornell is director of the Drake Memorial Library and Peter Olevnik is head of reference and coordinator of library instruction.

History. During the early 1970s emphasis was on course-related library instruction, which was provided in the form of class lectures as requested by faculty. In 1975–1976, a comprehensive library instruction program was developed and implemented using a three-phase, media-assisted approach (Olevnik, 1976). In 1980, the university developed a general education program. The library became involved in this planning process and was able to incorporate library instruction into the general education program.

Current Program Description. The library instruction program is a two-phase program and is part of two freshman communication skills courses, COM 111 and COM 112. In phase one, students in COM 111 are taught basic library skills on a self-instructional basis using videotapes and a workbook that includes a number of exercises (Gratch and others, 1981). During the second phase in COM 112, students apply previously learned skills to work on search strategies and to complete the workbook. Throughout their library work, all public services librarians assist students and review their programs. Approximately 1,000 students are involved in this program annually. The library instruction program has been developed, and continues to be reviewed, by librarians working in close cooperation with the faculty.

University of Colorado

The University of Colorado in Boulder, Colorado, is a large, comprehensive state university offering more than 120 fields of study through sixteen schools and colleges. In has an enrollment of 21,000 students. The University's libraries, including the Norlin Library and six branches, hold approximately four million volumes. The director of the Universities Libraries is Clyde Walton; Deborah Fink, reference and instruction librarian, is responsible for the reference department's bibliographic instruction program.

History. Library instruction has been a part of library services within the University of Colorado libraries for a long time. Documentation for these instructional activities is available since 1966. Credit courses such as Bibliography in the Humanities, Social Sciences, and Sciences were established in the early 1960s. From 1960 to 1971 many of the bibliographic instruction efforts originated within the college library; these efforts included tours, handbooks, programmed texts, and a slide-tape program as well as lectures to classes by the reference department. In 1971 the Term Paper Clinic for undergraduates and Dissertation Acupuncture for Ph.D. candidates were initiated and various miniguides (later these became "Data Grabs") to reference sources were developed. A five-year grant from the Council on Library Resources and the National Endowment for the Humanities was received for 1973-1978 to improve and increase student and faculty involvement in library use; these grants helped create two half-time positions for librarians in the history and economics departments. Under the grant program, extensive evaluation criteria for bibliographic instruction was developed (Lubans, 1974; Edwards, 1977; LaBue, 1977). The library skills credit course, Bibliography 301, continued to be successful and doubled its enrollment in 1978-1979. Individual instructional help offered by the reference department continued to increase.

Current Program Description. The bibliographic instruction program at the University of Colorado teaches students research skills by using various formats:

1. At the request of faculty, librarians teach classes in library use skills and demonstrate search strategy. A philosophy and set of objectives have been developed for these lectures; transparencies, a variety of handouts, and two slide-tape programs are used in instruction Approximately 215 sessions are provided to 3,650 students annually. Short evaluations of these class sessions are part of the program.
2. A two-hour credit course, Bibliography 301, is offered each semester and teaches students the steps of researching a topic without students actually having to write a paper. Enrollment has been increasing; two sections are now offered each semester. Other credit courses in library use are offered through the business, law, and music libraries.
3. The Term Paper Assistance Program is offered each semester for students who have special research needs related to a library assignment. One hundred to two hundred students take advantage of this program each year.
4. Graduate research workshops for writers of theses and dissertations

are offered. They involve a series of eight sessions of one and one-half hour each and participants must register for the workshops. Evaluations from participants have been used to revise these workshops.

5. The reference department's reference referral service offers individualized instruction (on a sign up basis) in library use. The library staff has continued to develop, revise, and update a series of handouts, "Data Grabs," for use in classes and by individuals.

It is noteworthy that the reference department's annual instructional contact hours have continued to increase from the lowest in 1979–1980 (1,166 contact hours) to a high of 6,180 contact hours in 1981–1982.

The reference instruction librarian works closely with the reference department staff and the Library Use Instruction Committee to coordinate and develop bibliographic instruction activities.

University of Texas at Austin

The University of Texas at Austin, located in Austin, Texas, is a large, comprehensive universtiy offering a wide variety of degree programs from various schools and colleges and has an enrollment of 45,000 students. The library system contains collections in more than twenty libraries among which are the Main (Perry-Casteneda) Library and the Undergraduate Library, with four and a half million volumes. The director libraries is Harold Billings and Barbara A. Schwartz is the coordinator of the instructional program in the Undergraduate Library.

History. In 1975, the undergraduate library staff and the freshman English instructional staff at the University of Texas at Austin began the development and implementation of a course-related library instruction program for all freshmen. The program utilized a unique combination of self-paced and course-related instruction designed to reach 8,000 freshmen in 150 sections each year (Dyson, 1978). Goals and objectives as well as a philosophy of user instruction were developed to emphasize the library's teaching function. Library tasks and responsibilities were reorganized to use staff more effectively for bibliographic instruction. Instructional materials in print and in audio-visual format were utilized for the course-integrated bibliographic instruction program in freshman English. These materials included a self-guided tour, study guides, exercises, and point-of-use aids that were developed and revised each year based on changing needs (Schwartz and Burton, 1981).

Current Program Description. The University of Texas at Austin continues to teach library skills to freshmen in English on a comprehensive course-integrated basis. Five hundred forty-four sections, which include 13,600 students of freshman English, receive instruction annually. Three librarians, including the coordinator, devote half of their time to this program while the rest of the undergraduate library staff supports the program with reference- and collection-development activities. Individualized instruction utilizing printed materials is followed up by individualized reference help from librarians and library assistants throughout the six to eight weeks required to complete the library unit. Close cooperation with the English classroom faculty has encouraged students to rely on faculty, rather than librarians, to introduce basic library skills. Formative and summative evaluations are used to improve the program and to assess the long-term impact of teaching library skills to freshman English students.

In addition, instruction is provided to sophomore level English classes through study guides on literary criticisms, and a library component is included in the multisectioned (1,471 students) sophomore level technical writing course. In technical writing, students are given subject research information appropriate to their major (business, engineering, life sciences, computer sciences, or nursing). Follow-up reference services for these students is provided by librarians in the main library and other branch libraries. Additionally, traditional, course-related library instruction takes place throughout the university.

University of Toronto

The University of Toronto, Ontario, Canada, is a large, comprehensive university offering a wide variety of degrees from various colleges and schools and has an enrollment of 50,000 students. The library collections (five and one-half million volumes) are housed in more than thirty campus libraries. The main library includes, among others, the J. P. Roberts Research Library, the Sigmund Samuel Undergraduate Library and the Science and Medicine Library. The director of the library is Marilyn Sharrow and the coordinator of library instruction is Carolyn Murray.

History. The first orientation librarian position was created in 1972, the Roberts Library was opened in 1973, and the coordinator of library instruction position was created in 1976. Since 1976, goals and objectives have been developed to aid in planning the library instruction program; a study skills component was added to this program in 1981.

Current Program Description. The main basis of the instruction program is regularly scheduled sessions (paper and essay clinics) in which students participate outside of the classroom. Thirty-nine percent of the total number of students who receive library instruction participate in these sessions annually while the other 61 percent receive library instruction through course-related instruction, which involves an average of 225 class sessions annually. Special sessions for graduate students are also offered.

The newest addition to the instruction program, study skills sessions in cooperation with the University's Advisory Bureau's Study Skills program, provided library skills to 800 students in twenty sessions the first year.

Much of the emphasis (50 percent) of the library instruction program is on the production of instructional print materials including point-of-use aids, brochures, signs, library guides, instructional handouts, and audiovisual aids. A wide variety of these guides and self-instructional materials are available to those interested in the program.

To increase librarians' expertise in teaching in the library instruction program, several activities are regularly scheduled. Workshops are held on campus so that librarians can address specific areas of concern related to library instruction. In addition, librarians are encouraged to attend national workshops and conferences; also, peer assessments of individual librarian's teaching skills take place on a regular basis.

Spot evaluations by participants in the paper and essay clinics have also been occasionally performed.

In addition to library instruction for university students, the library instruction program also provides tours and instructional sessions for large numbers of nonuniversity groups and individuals.

University of Wisconsin at Parkside

University of Wisconsin at Parkside, located in Kenosha, Wisconsin, is a young, urban commuter campus within the University of Wisconsin System and has an enrollment of 5,800 students, many of whom are nontraditional. The university offers programs in the traditional liberal arts as well as science and engineering. Master's programs in business and public administration are also available. The faculty are teachers and scholars and are heavily involved in research projects. The director of the library and learning center is Hannelore B. Rader and Judith Pryor is the coordinator of instruction. All seven public services staff members are involved in the instruction program.

History. Since 1973, the library has evolved as a teaching library by becoming more involved in the teaching and learning process on campus. Development of goals and objectives has been encouraged and plays an important role in the budget planning process. Similar to the Earlham College program, the University of Wisconsin at Parkside library instruction program began on a small scale and has continued to grow.

Current Program Description. The library instruction program has developed a set of goals and objectives; the program has several levels, from the basic library skills competency requirement to advanced course-integrated instruction in specific subject areas. The program's philosophy is that all students need certain basic and advanced bibliographic and information searching skills to survive as students and members of the community. Thus, students should be able to identify and use major resources of an academic or a public library. They should learn research strategies and techniques. Library instruction is carried out using a basic skills workbook as well as advanced subject workbooks, lectures, exercises, and other printed guides. All librarians also participate in the faculty liaison project that involve faculty in collection development, in assessing library-related needs in each discipline. This project also functions to provide faculty with research help (including on-line searching), to stimulate the expansion of bibliographic instruction, and to accomplish a number of cultural outreach activities. Thus, University of Wisconsin at Parkside tries to emulate an expanded model of the teaching library (Guskin and others, 1979). Faculty are beginning to realize the contributions the teaching library can make to the teaching and learning process on the campus. Both students and faculty have become more effective in the teaching and learning process in areas involving library-related assignments and library-related research work.

Winthrop College

Winthrop College, located in Rock Hill, South Carolina, is an established, state-supported college offering programs for undergraduate and graduate students in education, business, and arts and sciences. It has an enrollment of 5,000 students. Shirley M. Tarlton is dean of library services and Nancy Davidson is coordinator of bibliographic instruction.

History. Library use instruction has been in existence in some form since 1915 when regular classes on library skills were taught to some 700 students. By 1945, all freshman and transfer students were required to take six library lectures, which were followed by a test. In 1949–1950, four library lessons were provided during orientation week and were followed by a test. During 1958, library instruction was incorporated into several English classes, and this marked the beginning of course-related bibliographic instruction at Winthrop College. From the 1950s to 1969, library instruction was given to most students and all students had to pass a library test. A number of different approaches to library instruction were tried in the 1960s to make the instruction more effective. By 1971, a new library had been built, two new public service positions were added, and the instruction program was revised. A self-guided tour exercise and library guide were developed to help students develop research skills. In 1976–1977, library instruction became a requirement for English 101, and questions about the library became part of the midterm exam. In 1977–1978 library instruction became a regular component of English 102. Course-related instruction continued to grow, and goals and objectives for bibliographic instruction were developed.

Current Program Description. The bibliographic instruction program at Winthrop College has several levels. A tape tour orients students to facilities and services. Freshmen students in Writing 101 have two library sessions that teach appropriate search strategies through completion of a pathfinder in order to aid students in preparing term papers.

In addition, librarians provide course-related instruction in various subjects for undergraduate and graduate students. One hundred seventy-five sessions for approximately 3,570 students are given annually.

All eleven librarians participate in the bibliographic instruction program. Technical services librarians teach one-fifth of the total sessions. Bibliographies, the Dacus Library Guide, transparencies, exercises, and pathfinders are revised and new ones are prepared each year.

Continuing close cooperation with faculty is leading to increased demands for course-related instruction. The library staff has sponsored workshops for faculty to encourage them to incorporate basic writing and library skills into their subject content areas. The workshops have helped faculty develop specific procedures and strategies to teach research and library skills.

Summary

While the eleven programs described meet most of the criteria outlined at the beginning of this chapter, there are a number of other noteworthy bibliographic instruction programs in the United States and Canada that could also be included in this list. While the bibliographic instruction programs vary tremendously, all of them have a number of factors in common: (1) they are based on assessed user and campus needs and available resources, (2) they are built around goals and objectives, (3) they are comprehensive and multilevel and use a variety of instructional methods and materials, (4) they have been around for more than five years, (5) they have continued to change as needs changed, (6) they have grown each year, and (5) most importantly, they are having an impact on each campus.

Program Impact on the Campus. Close and continuous cooperation between librarians and classroom faculty has produced a different teaching and learning environment on campus and has also begun to result in the first real curriculum integrated library instruction. Faculty are beginning to find out what librarians can contribute to the education of students and how librarians' expertise in the bibliographic area can enrich teaching styles. Curriculum revisions and changes in the 1970s have helped librarians become more involved in curriculum planning and promote bibliographic instruction.

Students are profiting immensely from these bibliographic instruction programs. They are learning basic and advanced library skills on a systematic basis and are becoming more skilled at research and term projects. Students are also acquiring much-needed life-long information seeking skills that often include computer-related skills (on-line data base searching, familiarity with on-line catalogue and circulation systems, and microcomputer skills).

The impact of the bibliographic instruction programs on campus administrators has been to make them aware of how rich and important a resource their campus libraries really are. This, in turn, can result in increased support for the library. The library that is involved in library instruction programs is viewed as innovative and even as a change agent. Since most of the programs have been accomplished with no or few additional resources, administrators are impressed with the endeavor.

Program Impact on the Library. The impact of the bibliographic instruction program on the library is many-faceted. Use of the library tends to increase dramatically as more faculty and students become converted to the idea of library skills instruction. This growth, coupled with the increased use of the library facility and services, tends to be a burden for the staff after awhile. Continuous staff training and development is necessary to continue staff performance at high levels in the instruction program in order to offer good follow-up reference service. Cooperation and communication among the entire library staff has to be a priority. Occasionally, there are problems caused by resistance to the bibliographic instruction program and these must be carefully addressed. Personnel shortages related to budget problems seem to be among the most common of these. One of the most gratifying facts emerging from the programs described here is that bibliographic instruction can be a successful program in any type of institution, whether small, medium-sized, or large, and it can be accomplished with existing resources.

References

Atkins, T., and Langstaff, E. *Access to Information: Library Research Methods.* Elmsford, N.Y.: Collegium Press, 1979.

Dyson, A. J. "Library Instruction in University Undergraduate Libraries." In J. Lubans, Jr., (Ed.), *Progress in Educating the Library User.* New York: Bowker, 1978.

Edwards, S. "Library Use Studies and the University of Colorado." In H. Rader (Ed.), *Library Instruction in the Seventies: State of the Art.* Ann Arbor: Pierian Press, 1977.

Farber, E. I. "Library Instruction Throughout the Curriculum: Earlham College Program." In J. Lubans (Ed.), *Educating the Library User.* New York: Bowker, 1974.

Gratch, B., and others. *Getting There from Here: A Media-Assisted Library Instruction Program for All Freshman Students in Communication Skills Courses.* ERIC Document Reproduction Service, 1981. ED 208 837.

Guskin, A. E., Stoffle, C. J., and Boisse, J. A. "The Academic Library as a Teaching Library: A Role for the 1980s." *Library Trends,* 1979, *28,* 281–296.

Hughes, P., and Flandreau, A. "Tutorial Library Instruction: The Freshman Program at Berea College." *Journal of Academic Librarianship,* 1980, *6,* 91–94.

Kennedy, J. K., Jr. "Integrated Library Instruction." *Library Journal,* 1970, *95,* 1450–1453.

Kennedy, J. R., Kirk, T. G., and Weaver, G. A. "Course-Related Library Instruction: A Case Study of the English and Biology Departments at Earlham College." *Drexel Library Quarterly,* 1971, *7,* 277–297.

Kerker, S., Murray, D., and Robbins, A. "LIP Service: The Undergraduate Library Instruction Program at The Ohio State University." *Journal of Academic Librarianship,* 1981, *7,* 279–282.

LaBue, B. "Evaluating Faculty Involvement in Library Instruction" In H. Rader (Ed.), *Library Instruction in the Seventies: State of the Art.* Ann Arbor: Pierian Press, 1977.

Lee, J. H. "Instruction, Communication and the Faculty." In C. Kirkendall (Ed.), *Reform and Renewal in Higher Education: Implications for Library Instruction.* Ann Arbor: Pierian Press, 1980.

Lee, J. H., and Miller, A. H., Jr. "Introducing On Line Data Base Searching in the Small Academic Library: A Model for Service Without Charge to Undergraduates." *Journal of Academic Librarianship,* 1981, *7,* 14–22.

Lubans, J., Jr. "Evaluating Library-User Education Programs." In J. Lubans, Jr. (Ed.), *Educating the Library User.* New York: Bowker, 1974.

Olevnik, P. P. *A Media-Assisted Library Instruction Orientation Program Report.* ERIC Document Reproduction Service, 1976. ED 134 138.

Pearson, P., and Tiefel, V. "Evaluating Undergraduate Library Instruction at the Ohio State University." *Journal of Academic Librarianship,* 1982, *7,* 351–357.

Rader, H. B. *An Assessment of Ten Academic Library Instruction Programs in the United States and Canada.* ERIC Document Reproduction Service, 1976. ED 171 276.

Rothstein, P. M., and McDonough, K. "Library Teaching Packages: Project Development and Evaluation." *Education Libraries,* 1982, *7,* 54–56.

Schwartz, B. A., and Burton, S. *Teaching Library Skills in Freshman English: An Undergraduate Library's Experience.* Austin: The General Libraries, University of Texas at Austin, 1981.

University Survey: A Guidebook for New Students. Columbus, Ohio: University College, 1982.

Hannelore B. Rader is director of the Library/Learning Center at the University of Wisconsin at Parkside, Kenosha. She has written and spoken widely on bibliographic instruction and was instrumental in the development of the instruction program at Eastern Michigan University.

*Through sharing the results of successful bibliographic instruction
programs, the national LOEX clearinghouse can provide vital
assistance to librarians participating in the teaching mission
of their institution.*

Improving Teaching:
How a Clearinghouse Helps

Carolyn A. Kirkendall

Bibliographic instruction (BI) is widely recognized in the United States as a
legitimate and integral component of an academic library's total public service
program. In tracing the ups and downs of recent bibliographic instruction
activity in academic libraries, a decline in the effectiveness of instruction programs occurred in the 1950s, and a resurgence that provided the roots for
today's peak of activity started again in the late 1960s. Perhaps the most
important reason for this renewed and continuing activity is that academic
librarians collectively and simultaneously became dissatisfied with the appar-
ent appalling lack of students' skills in conducting library research and knowledge of the library collection.

These practitioners recognized that the academic library—and academic librarians—had a potentially valuable instructional role in the curriculum. Bibliographic instruction, as offered as a part of the total reference service program, could support the teaching faculty member's work and also provide more varied assignments. Such a program would help develop more self-
sufficient library users and increase library use.

Background of LOEX

The idea of establishing a central clearinghouse agency to collect and
share both sample library orientation materials and the data from these programs was conceived at the First Conference on Library Orientation for Aca-

T. G. Kirk (Ed.). *Increasing the Teaching Role of Academic Libraries.*
New Directions for Teaching and Learning, no. 18. San Francisco: Jossey-Bass, June 1984.

demic Librarians in 1971. Practitioners realized they could not individually keep up with the increased and flourishing library orientation and instruction program activities. They were also concerned about the duplication of effort and material that was occurring in library instruction programs across the country.

In 1972, Project LOEX (library orientation exchange) became a reality. After receiving financial support from the Council on Library Resources during the growing years of clearinghouse activity, the national LOEX office at Eastern Michigan University now operates as a self-supporting agency and continues to function as a central exchange for bibliographic instruction programs on a nationwide basis. The growing commitment of school, public, and special librarians to improve their bibliographic instruction offerings has resulted in the recent expansion of the LOEX office's service to collect data and samples from environments other than college and university sources. As the number of library instruction programs in colleges and universities continues to grow, so does the clearinghouse's collection of materials and data base information. Over 2,000 institutions have contacted the exchange during the past decade; over 25,000 sample materials produced by academic libraries to teach library skills within the institutional curriculum have been deposited. In response to the 12,356 requests received by LOEX since the clearinghouse became operational, over 81,000 copies of sample materials have been circulated.

Present Services and Activities

Through the provision of typical clearinghouse services, the LOEX exchange provides assistance in a variety of ways to librarians in developing instruction programs and thus supports the role that librarians can play in providing learning assistance. By collecting, organizing, and sharing information and materials, clearinghouses eliminate costly duplication, save time and effort, and provide a forum of communication among individuals interested in a common subject.

Providing Information. The LOEX *News*, an informal quarterly newsletter, provides a national forum for the exchange of ideas and information. Regular features of the newsletter include: (1) letters to the editor; (2) a list of publications available for purchase; (3) a bibliography of pertinent articles, monographs, and ERIC documents; (4) a list of upcoming meetings and conferences related to user education; (5) a section on activities of bibliographic instruction committees, groups, and state and regional clearinghouses; (6) highlights of the most interesting and useful contributions recently received at the LOEX office and available on loan; and (7) current news in the field. Library journals are scanned on a regular basis for additional interesting features and information to include.

Since 1974, issues of the *News* have also included additional details of programs and activities to illustrate "who's doing what, and can help you do it too," which is the newsletter's stated purpose. For example, the following features have been published in the *News*:

- New documents received
- Requests for specific kinds of instructional material
- Requests for information or help for work in progress
- Reviews of worthwhile publications
- Summaries of conferences and speeches
- Calls for papers
- Promotion of the formulation of standards and guidelines
- Encouragement of growth of committees within professional organizations
- Encouragement of changes in library school curricula
- Lists of job openings
- Publication of the "ideal" job description
- Editorials
- Staffing programs
- Clearinghouse progress and statistical reports
- Announcements of BI grants received
- Details of available grants
- Policy statements
- International news

LOEX also serves as an information forum in several additional ways. Directories of programs that list activities and their scope are compiled by the office. Sample materials are collected that illustrate the ways these programs are implemented. Directories of practitioners in various subject disciplines are also kept current since much of the work of a clearinghouse involves referrals. By providing contact names of those working in the same area as the enquirer, LOEX helps to broaden the base of potential information sources a clearinghouse client can use. Both these directories are compiled from the circulation of questionnaires, through conversation, and by a great deal of correspondence. In the past decade, the LOEX office sent over 9,000 letters of enquiry or response (excluding letters and replies sent along with loan materials).

While most of the LOEX exchange procedures are carried out by mail, participation in workshops, seminars, and conferences has greatly assisted in the provision of bibliographic instruction information to others. Each May, the LOEX office has sponsored an Annual Library Instruction Conference or Workshop. Published proceedings of the conferences are available through commercial distribution (see Phillips, this volume).

Sharing Materials. LOEX was established to provide a mechanism for sharing documents that are related to the scope of the clearinghouse. Physical accessibility to the materials in the files is, for most librarians throughout the country, impossible. Therefore, much of the LOEX program's attention is directed to processing and sharing sample items through the mail. Borrowers can copy the samples which LOEX has collected and organized and must return the borrowed materials after one week's use. The clearinghouse collects two to three copies of each item so that the frustration of waiting to receive circulating samples can be somewhat alleviated. Borrowers are requested to give credit to the originating institution when they modify and adapt a sample handout for their own particular usage.

Document distribution also occurs through specially prepared exhibits of bibliographic instruction materials. LOEX provides these displays for use at conferences and meetings throughout the year in the United States and Canada and tailors them to the specific topic of library instruction on which the meeting may be focused. Discipline-related exhibits and displays are also compiled.

Additional Services. Besides the sharing of information and instructional materials, a clearinghouse can also provide additional services. By using the data and samples on hand, LOEX assists librarians in their cooperative teaching and learning role through the compilation of research reports. Many librarians call upon the exchange to provide statistics about library instruction in colleges and universities for use in promoting their own programs. For example, when librarians are interested in developing a workbook on library skills to use in the English curriculum at their local institution, LOEX can provide details of other institutions that have already implemented workbook programs, required workbook units, colleges that have discarded this method of user education, or the type of information that should be included in the typical workbook.

The compilation of bibliographies has been another LOEX service that has been continually provided during the past ten years. The professional literature is filled with bibliographic instruction articles, and thus an annual listing is not always directly helpful. The LOEX exchange provides free copies of subject, topic, and format bibliographies on request and keeps each listing current.

An important clearinghouse service that has evolved during the past decade has been the provision of advice. After years of operation, the program has a clear idea of what is needed in a bibliographic instruction program and what might be changed. These opinions can be shared on the consultative level when requested. Perhaps one of the reasons that the LOEX agency has continued to garner support, financial backing, and cooperation is because samples and programs are not intentionally judged or rated one against the other. All contributions play a vital role in making the LOEX collection a representative one. A decade ago, and even today, librarians developing their own programs and materials might be reluctant to share their opinions and to record the results of their often informal, in-house experimental work, especially if they feared their efforts would be used as examples of "how not to do it." Actually, such experiences are most valuable and, fortunately, many libraries currently do contribute materials and information about those projects that turned out not to be appropriate or successful.

The British Experience

It is useful, when reviewing LOEX services, to compare them with the user education clearinghouse established in the United Kingdom in 1977. The need for an information officer for user education was also recognized as a need by the British office, although for somewhat different reasons than the LOEX office. The position at this office was identified as a means to rationalize and exploit ongoing programs.

The British agency differs from the LOEX exchange in several ways. The position of the information officer is funded by the British library, as is a series of ongoing library user education projects in the United Kingdom. Samples are mailed out for retention, not on loan. The officer makes on-site visits to collect information, an enviable but impossible task for an American clearinghouse director. (There are over 3,000 academic libraries in the United States, while in the United Kingdom there are under 100 institutions of higher education.) LOEX must collect information through questionnaire, conversation, and correspondence.

The British agency, moreover, publishes and sells bibliographies and study reports. In the United States, the widespread publication of top-quality monographs on bibliographic instruction recently solved the problem of distributing information about bibliographic instruction; however, the LOEX exchange could, in the future, produce kits and units on various methods and situations for purchase and could also produce exhibits and promotional materials that librarians could purchase for use in their particular situations. The market for these kinds of products appears to be good, and through the distribution of these materials, librarians would be better able to fulfill some of their bibliographic instruction responsibilities.

Observations and Recommended Programs

Curriculum-Related Programs. Whichever formats and approaches are used in teaching library skills, there is general agreement that they must relate to the curriculum and that the actual realm and future of these course-related, assignment-related programs are determined by the teaching faculty. For programs to be successful there must be cooperation both in spirit and fact. While it is commonly espoused that knowing how to find and use information is a goal of the educated person, it requires motivation of the person being educated to use good information-seeking procedures. Students whose grades depend on effective library use are more likely to take library use instruction seriously.

Discipline-Related Instruction. Hopkins (1981) has pointed out that subject-tailored, discipline-related classroom presentations by teaching librarians are predominantly the kind of group bibliographic instruction provided today. The number of these subject-related sessions has steadily increased, providing evidence that the concentration on basic, elemental library skills instruction characteristic of many programs is not necessary. The focus lately has turned to approaches that are more closely tied to the content and methodologies of various academic fields and to particular teaching and learning problems that occur in these fields. Again, the librarian in these situations is supporting the teaching faculty member and the course plan and therefore fulfilling the teaching role.

Administrative Support. The past decade has seen much refinement of programs and theories and has brought quality, discipline-related bibliographic instruction services to the fore on many campuses. These services will not be recognized as essential unless university and college administrators support them. Moffett (1982) laments the general lack of appreciation that administrators have shown for the library's role by quoting a librarian from a midwest university whose opinion many share: "The dean or vice-president of academic administration who understands college and/or university libraries is a very rare specimen" (p. 46). The library's presence is accepted as a given, but it is not seen as a vital resource for the intellectual endeavors of the institution.

Here is where the teaching role of the library can make an impact by influencing such thinking. Libraries can be seen as more cost-effective if ongoing, integrated instructional activity creates increased library use and initiates conversation among faculty on the value of the instructional support that these programs provide.

References

Hopkins, F. L. "User Instruction in the College Library: Origins, Prospects and a Practical Program." In W. Miller and S. Rockwood (Eds.), *College Librarianship.* Metuchen, N.J.: Scarecrow Press, 1981.

Moffett, W. A. "Don't Shelve Your College Librarian." *Educational Record,* 1982, *63,* 46–49.

Carolyn A. Kirkendall has, since 1975, been director of the national Library Orientation/Instruction Clearinghouse Exchange (LOEX) located at Eastern Michigan University. She has written and spoken widely on LOEX and on the state of bibliographic instruction.

A guide to the literature of bibliographic instruction combines
the listing of specific sources with recommendations for subject
access, personal contact, and current awareness.

More Information: Bibliographic
Instruction Resources

Linda L. Phillips

This chapter is intended to serve both the casual reader and the serious
researcher as a guide that lists personal contact that will provide additional
materials. The format of the guide is intended to retain currency while indicat-
ing how to find the most significant bibliographic resources available.

Bibliographic Instruction: State of the Art

Scrivener, J. E. "Instruction in Library Use: The Persisting Problem." *Austral-*
ian Academic and Research Libraries, 1982, *3* (2), 87–119.
    Scrivener's article remains the most comprehensive, brief, and current
description of bibliographic instruction programs and approaches.

Rader, H. B. (Ed.). *Library Instruction in the Seventies: State of the Art.* Papers presented at the Sixth Annual Conference on Library Orientation for Academic
Libraries held at Eastern Michigan University, May 13-14, 1976. Ann
Arbor: Pierian Press, 1977.
    Rader brings bibliographic instruction state of the art through the mid-
seventies. Papers in her collection summarize developments in course-related
instruction, credit courses and workbooks, evaluation of faculty involvement,
and international activity.

Lubans, J., Jr. (Ed.). *Educating the Library User.* New York: Bowker, 1974.
    Lubans presents a third review of the literature.

T. G. Kirk (Ed.). *Increasing the Teaching Role of Academic Libraries.*
New Directions for Teaching and Learning, no. 18. San Francisco: Jossey-Bass, June 1984.

Lubans, J., Jr. (Ed.). *Progress in Educating the Library User.* New York: Bowker, 1974.

The review article by Arthur P. Young (pp. 1–15) covers selected publications from 1930 to 1973. Young and Exir B. Brennan published a subsequent article covering the period from 1973 to 1978 (pp. 13–28) in Luban's book.

Marshall, A. P. (Ed.). "Current Library Use Instruction." *Library Trends,* 1980, *29* (1).

This article provides notable, state-of-the-art information.

Bibliographies

Bibliographies, although less descriptive than literature reviews, provide a comprehensive picture of bibliographic instruction development and its present status.

Lockwood, D. L. (Comp.). *Library Instruction: A Bibliography.* Westport, Conn: Greenwood Press, 1979.

Lockwood gives particular attention to materials published since 1970.

Lubans, J., Jr. (Ed.). *Educating the Library User.* New York: Bowker, 1974.

Lubans includes a bibliography (pp. 423–435) which refers to some of the best bibliographic instruction literature.

Krier, M. "Bibliographic Instruction: A Checklist of the Literature, 1931–1975." *Reference Services Review,* 1976, *4* (1), 7–31.

Krier provides a checklist of literature published from 1931 to 1975. Because of the extensive indexing, it is a good tool for identifying one or two items on a particular institution's program, methods of instruction, or instruction in subject fields.

Rader, H. B. "Library Orientation and Instruction — 1973: An Annotated Review of the Literature." *Reference Services Review,* 1974, *2* (1), 91–93. (Subsequent reviews appear in the following issues of *Reference Services Review:* 1975, *3* (1), 29–31; 1976, *4* (4), 91–93; 1977, *5* (1), 41–44; 1978, *6* (1), 45–51; 1979, *7* (1), 45–56; 1980, *8* (1), 31–46; 1981, *9* (2), 79–89; 1982, *10* (2), 33–41.

Rader has prepared an annual annotated bibliography of current resources that is useful for retrospective searching as well as for current bibliographic instruction awareness.

Subject Access to Bibliographic Instruction Literature

Both library catalogues and periodical indexes place most bibliographic instruction entries under general subject headings. The *Library of Congress Sub-*

ject Headings provides a network of possible headings to use. The most relevant subject heading for bibliographic instruction in academic libraries is:

> Library Orientation

Related terms do lead to other sources:

> College Students–Library Orientation
> Libraries–Handbooks, Manuals, etc.

Some broader headings require the use of subdivisions and careful perusal of book titles by the researcher:

> Libraries and Readers
> Libraries and Students
> Libraries, University and College
> Library Education

A subject heading which is gaining relevance reflects the need for training library users to find information with the help of computers:

> On-Line Bibliographic Searching

The subject search will produce numerous citations; one classic work that should be read and studied early in the quest for understanding of the literature, and that provides the philosophical basis for many bibliographic instruction efforts is:

Knapp, P. *The Monteith College Library Experiment.* New York: Scarecrow Press, 1966.

Knapp defined a program and attempted to practice a concept which established the librarian as a classroom partner with the teaching faculty.

For access to periodical literature *Library Literature* is the premier index. The most relevant heading to use is:

> Instruction in Library Use

Another productive term is:

> Library–College Concept

Related terms which may turn up additional articles include the following:

> Bibliography–Teaching
> Information Storage and Retrieval–Teaching
> Research and the Library
> Research Techniques
> Searching, Bibliographical
> Searching, Computer
> Surveys–Instruction in Library Use

Periodical literature in education complements that of the library journals. The most relevant *Education Index* heading to use is:

Libraries–Instruction in Use

Another possibility is the related term:

Reference Books–Teaching

The *Thesaurus of ERIC Descriptors* (9th ed., Phoenix, Ariz.: Oryx Press, 1982) gives terms which may be used to locate articles in *Current Index to Journals in Education.* The most relevant ERIC term is:

Library Instruction

Related subjects include the following:

Information Needs
Information Seeking
Libraries
Library Guides
Library Skills
Orientation Materials
Reference Materials
Research Tools
Search Strategies

Additional periodical indexes which might prove helpful are *Library and Information Science Abstracts,* which provides an international scope, and *Social Sciences Citation Index,* where indexing is by key word only and some book chapters are included.

Developing a Bibliographic Instruction Program

Readers interested in program development may want to cut across the historical, theoretical, and many applied works of the general literature to bring together information specifically focused on the steps necessary to planning and initiating a program. An earlier chapter in this volume provides descriptions of some of the most prominent programs. A variety of sources offer sound, step-by-step advice for developing a program well-suited to the local situation.

Association of College and Research Libraries, Bibliographic Instruction Section, Policy and Planning Committee. *Bibliographic Instruction Handbook.* Chicago, Ill.: American Library Association, 1979.

The *BI Handbook* contains national guidelines, needs assessment checklist, administrative considerations, program timetable, model objectives statement, modes of instruction chart, glossary of terms, and a pathfinder for bibliographic instruction programs.

Beaubien, A. K., Hogan S. A., and George, M. W. *Learning the Library*. New York: Bowker, 1982.

A how-to companion to Oberman and Strauch (below), this book covers setting objectives and selecting instructional modes within the parameters of the individual library community. The authors emphasize the importance of the structure of the literature within a discipline as a key to the research process. The book describes factors to consider for implementation of a bibliographic instruction program and includes a bibliography and an index.

Oberman, C., and Strauch, K. (Eds.). *Theories of Bibliographic Education: Designs for Teaching*. New York: Bowker, 1982.

This work takes a theoretical approach. It contains essays on issues such as teaching problem solving through research, teaching information structure, and teaching research in the context of the discipline. It includes a bibliography and an index.

Bolner, M. (Ed.). *Planning and Developing a Library Orientation Program*. Proceedings of the Third Annual Conference on Library Orientation for Academic Libraries, Eastern Michigan University, May 3-4, 1973. Ann Arbor, Mich: Pierian Press, 1975.

Papers include ideas for program design, making campus contacts, use of audiovisual materials, methods of instruction, and evaluation.

Kirk, T. G., Kennedy, J. R., Jr., and Van Zant, N. P. "Structuring Services and Facilities for Library Instruction." *Library Trends*, 1980, *29* (1), 39–53.

This bibliographic essay focuses on needed services and facilities for an effective bibliographic instruction program. The authors concentrate on publications from 1973 to 1979.

Renford, B., and Hendrickson, L. *Bibliographic Instruction: A Handbook*. New York: Neal-Schuman Publishers, Inc., 1980.

This book is a how-to-guide that covers steps for planning a program; various types of instructional tools such as printed guides and workbooks; and definition and analysis of course-related, credit, and computer-assisted instruction. The appendix on additional information sources contains lists of library instruction clearinghouses, newsletters, and professional organizations. The work includes a bibliography, glossary, and index.

Rice, J., Jr. *Teaching Library Use: A Guide for Library Instruction*. Westport, Conn.: Greenwood Press, 1981.

Another how-to guide, this book covers planning approaches to orientation and instruction, testing and evaluation, and physical facilities. The appendixes list annual conferences, sources and audiovisual materials, possible textbooks, and sources to help with test construction. It also includes a bibliography and an index.

Roberts, A. F. *Library Instruction for Librarians.* Littleton, Colo.: Libraries Unlimited, 1982.

This source is a textbook which includes background information, components of a bibliographic instruction plan, specific teaching techniques, modes of instruction, and methods for evaluation. Chapters contain numerous samples, exercises, and selected readings.

(Lockwood's book, cited in the bibliographic section above, contains many other useful sources for help with program development (pp. 13–28).

Specific Programs and Forms of Instruction

Hundreds of successful bibliographic instruction programs exist that incorporate multiple combinations of instructional forms. An earlier chapter in this issue provides descriptions of some of the most prominent programs. The literature contains descriptions of the best-known programs and methods of instruction; some significant works follow:

Werking, R. H. *The Library and the College: Some Programs of Library Instruction.* 1976. (ED 127 917)

Werking describes programs started by Harvie Branscomb, Louis Shores, Patricia Knapp, and Evan Farber.

Dudley, M. *Library Instruction Workbook: A Self-Directed Course in the Use of UCLA's College Library.* Los Angeles: College Library, University of California, 1981.

The original edition of this workbook inspired many adaptations for reaching large numbers of students.

The General Libraries. *A Comprehensive Program of User Education for the General Libraries, The University of Texas at Austin.* The General Libraries, University of Texas at Austin, 1977.

This document focuses on the background work done by University of Texas at Austin librarians to plan for a bibliographic instruction program; it includes copies of questionnaires sent to faculty and students with summary results, report forms for collecting information about existing activities, goals and objectives, and proposals for a comprehensive program.

Schwartz, B., and Burton, S. *Teaching Library Skills in Freshman English: An Undergraduate Library's Experience.* Austin: The General Libraries, The University of Texas at Austin, 1981

This thorough description of the program at a large research institution reveals the evolution of the University of Texas at Austin proposals into an integral part of the academic curriculum.

Farber, E. I. "Library Instruction Throughout the Curriculum: Earlham College Program." In J. Lubans (Ed.), *Educating the Library User.* New York: Bowker, 1974.

Stoffle, C. J., and Pryor, J. M. "Competency-Based Education and Library Instruction." *Library Trends,* 1980, *29* (1), 55–67.

The authors discuss competency-based programs at six diverse academic institutions, including the University of Wisconsin at Parkside, which has the most comprehensive program.

Support Groups

Once the bibliographic instruction practitioner or observer has reviewed the literature, support groups have much to offer in the way of personal contact, current information, and inspiration. The best-known and most active agency for sharing information is LOEX:

> Library Orientation — Instruction Exchange;
>   The National Clearinghouse for Library Use Instruction
> Center of Educational Resources
> Eastern Michigan University
> Ypsilanti, Michigan 48197

In addition to LOEX, three major American Library Association (ALA) groups vigorously promote bibliographic instruction through discussion of issues, political action within the organization, and dissemination of information. Described in the *ALA Handbook of Organization, 1982/83* (Chicago: American Library Association, 1982), the three groups are:

> Instruction in the Use of Libraries Committee, p. 13
> Library Instruction Round Table, p. 145
> Association of College and Research Libraries. Bibliographic Instruction Section, p. 53

Several other units exist within ALA, particularly among the discipline-related committees. Consult the *ALA Handbook* for a complete list. Both Lockwood (pp. 9–13) and Renford and Hendrickson (pp. 182–183) list more clearinghouses and professional organizations.

Keeping Current with Bibliographic Instruction

Staying abreast of new developments in any field presents a challenge. The literature contains several distinct avenues for those who wish to be well-informed. Since 1974, Hannelore Rader has published in *Reference Services Review* the annual, annotated bibliography of books and articles cited earlier in this chapter. Beginning in spring 1982, *Reference Services Review* launched a regular Rader column:

Rader, H. B. "Bibliographic Instruction." [Bibliographic Instruction in the 1980s]. *Reference Services Review,* 1982, *10* (1), 65–66.

Other columns in library journals are:

1. Kirkendall, C. "Library Instruction: A Column of Opinion." *Journal of Academic Librarianship*, 1976, *2* (4) to 1982, *8* (5).
   Kirkendall's column appears as the "Dialogue and Debate" feature in a new journal, *Research Strategies*, which began in early 1983.
2. Kirkendall, C. "A Review of the Past. . . A Call for the Future." *Research Strategies*, 1983, *1* (1).
3. Lubans, J., Jr. "Library Literacy." *RQ*, 1980, *19* (4).

The LOEX newsletter, mentioned previously, is an excellent source for keeping up with bibliographic instruction activities:

LOEX News: The Quarterly Newsletter of the Library Orientation-Instruction Exchange. Ypsilanti, Mich.: Center of Educational Resources, Eastern Michigan University, 1974.

Conferences constitute another valuable resource for information; many participants find equally worthwhile the conference program content and the opportunities for personal contacts with other specialists. Since 1971 the Annual Conference on Library Orientation for Academic Libraries has been held at Eastern Michigan University, with published proceedings following each year; since 1982 the conference has been help biennially. Bibliographic instruction groups within the American Library Association regularly present programs at the annual conference; the ALA midwinter conference affords participation in the exchange of ideas that help shape the summer programs. The ALA Association of College and Research Libraries has presented preconference programs for both annual and midwinter meetings. Also, numerous regional library conferences feature bibliographic instruction. For example, the 4th Southeastern Conference on Approaches to Bibliographic Instruction was held at the University of North Carolina at Charlotte in 1983.

Trends in the 1980s

Certain directions are evident as the field expands. In her opening *Reference Services Review* column on bibliographic instruction in the 1980s, Hannelore Rader (p. 65) noted several current trends:

- Growing use of workbooks
- More required library skills programs
- More interest in computer-assisted instruction
- More librarians using pre- and posttests for evaluation
- Increased popularity of instruction in the use of on-line data bases and catalogues.

Another trend, definition and promotion of the theoretical approach to bibliographic instruction with particular focus on differing structures of the literature by discipline, has appeared both in written form and in conference hallway discussion. Two representative articles include:

1. Hopkins, F. L. "A Century of Bibliographic Instruction: The Historical Claim to Professional and Academic Legitimacy." *College and Research Libraries,* 1982, *43* (3), 192–198.
2. Kobelski, P., and Reichel, M. "Conceptual Frameworks for Bibliographic Instruction." *Journal of Academic Librarianship,* 1981, *7* (2), 73–77.

In a related vein, librarians have been working to expand bibliographic instruction awareness into the various subject disciplines. The Association of College and Research Libraries (ACRL) has sponsored a liaison program to coordinate program proposals with various professional associations. Currently the LOEX clearinghouse director coordinates the program. Background information on the philosophy of this project may be found in:

Senzig, D. "Bibliographic Instruction in the Discipline Associations." *College and Research Libraries News,* 1980, *41* (10), 297–298.

For further trends one may read the research agenda submitted by the ACRL Bibliographic Instruction Section Research Committee that calls for study and experimentation in the areas of defining and measuring library skills, design and implementation of programs, and management aspects:

ACRL BIS Research Committee. "Research Agenda for Bibliographic Instruction." *College and Research Libraries News,* 1980, *41* (4), 94–95.

The BIS Research Committee recently completed an evaluation handbook:

Evaluating Bibliographic Instruction: A Handbook. Chicago: American Library Association, 1983.

Evaluation has long been an elusive issue; the handbook will provide more direction for an area where there has been uncertainty and inaction.

Finally, a group from BIS called the Think Tank met in the last few years and published an agenda which may well set trends for the rest of the decade:

American Library Association. Association of College and Research Libraries. Bibliographic Instruction Section. "Think Tank Recommendations for Bibliographic Instruction." *College and Research Libraries News,* 1981, *42* (11), 394–398.

Integration was one key theme; the Think Tank recommended building bridges to the library profession, academic community, and library schools. A second theme focused on the value of research and publication as a base for making bibliographic instruction a distinct discipline.

Conclusion

This guide has indicated key points for gaining access to bibliographic instruction literature. The path does not end here; the reader must select specific, needed information from the many resources available. The reader may now create new paths through study of the literature, reshaping of ideas after practice and discussion, and sharing new challenges with the academic community.

Linda L. Phillips is associate professor and head of the John C. Hodges Undergraduate Library Reference Department, University of Tennessee, Knoxville. She has developed and implemented bibliographic instruction programs for undergraduates at a two-year technical institute and at a large research institution.

*Why incorporate a bibliographic instruction program
into the liberal arts curriculum?*

Concluding Comments

Thomas G. Kirk

This volume has provided a full discussion of the concept of the teaching
library in general and specifically of bibliographic instruction. However, it has
not provided a defense of the need for such programs. What follows is a brief
argument that bibliographic instruction be an essential part of an undergraduate educational program.

A bibliographic instruction program can be justified on the practical
level since it meets the immediate needs of students. At best, students graduate from high school with a working knowledge of a high school library; they
will know the *Readers' Guide*, a card catalogue for a collection of several thou-
sand volumes, and such reference tools as a general encyclopedia and dictio-
nary. At worst students will brag that they got through high school without
using the library. Then, when students enter college, they are expected to
know how to use the vast array of subject encyclopedias, specialized bibliographies and other reference tools, and the card catalogue for a much larger collection. Furthermore, students will have access to a wide range of indexes
from the general *Humanities Index* to the more specialized indexes such as *Child
Development Abstracts and Bibliography* or *Energy Information Abstracts*.

But how will students learn to use these research tools? There are four
answers. The most likely, unfortunately, is they do not learn. Students will
continue to use the tried and true methods of high school—the card catalogue,
and, if the teacher insists on journal articles, the *Readers' Guide*. A second
answer is that the student learns by trial and error, expending many hours in

T. G. Kirk (Ed.). *Increasing the Teaching Role of Academic Libraries.*
New Directions for Teaching and Learning, no. 18. San Francisco: Jossey-Bass, June 1984.

95

frustrating attempts to make the library system work. Sometimes students are bold enough to ask a reference librarian for assistance, in which case they will get specific guidance on the problems at hand. However, the reference librarian can only provide a solution to an immediate problem. The fourth and most effective way students can learn is through systematic instruction in the use of reference sources and research techniques. This formal instruction does not fully eliminate the methods of trial and error or of asking the reference librarian for help. However, it avoids the problems of useless frustration, inconsistency, and failure to reach those students who most need the instruction. But perhaps, most importantly, this method delivers a message to students that faculty believe learning to use libraries efficiently and effectively is an important skill.

Bibliographic instruction can be more than providing directions on how to use library resources to complete a specific assignment. It can also make a significant contribution to the aims of liberal education. One of the most important functions of a liberal arts program is to develop those abilities and qualities that characterize the rational mind. This includes the ability to solve problems by asking questions, critically analyzing the information, and then answering the questions. While these skills can be learned without the use of library resources, students will only be able to realize the full potential of the skills learned if they have acquired the capacity to access information. With the ability to effectively manipulate bibliographic systems, the student is able to collect the relevant, timely, and authoritative information necessary to support the problem-solving process.

This ability to solve problems is important to the students' quality of life after college and to public discussion of issues in our society. Students with the ability to ask questions, gather and evaluate information, and answer those questions can remain active learners throughout life. They are able to respond positively to the challenges in their lives.

A liberal arts program also attempts to provide students with a thorough knowledge of a particular discipline. This coverage of a field of study includes the basic concepts of the field as well as its technical vocabulary. An additional aspect of the study of a discipline includes a scrutiny of how practitioners and researchers explore topics and contribute to the vocabulary and concepts which form the body of the discipline. Instruction in this aspect of the discipline is accomplished by such activities as student research projects. By an examination of a variety of research papers and an exposure to how experimental results are used to substantiate a conclusion or answer a question, the student gains understanding of the research process. Using the literature to solve problems in this way helps to provide a setting in which students must come to grips with the scholarly process.

It is hoped that the chapters in this sourcebook will make teaching faculty and administrators on college and university campuses more aware of the bibliographic instruction activities that are being provided by their own libraries and other academic libraries across the country. As an outgrowth of this awareness, librarians and teaching faculty can hopefully form a partnership in instruction that can help students fully realize the potential that libraries have for enriching and informing their lives both during college and after their formal education ends.

Thomas G. Kirk is college librarian at Berea College, Berea, Kentucky.

Index